Sociology of
Families &
Households

Jill Swale

Advanced
Topic*Master*

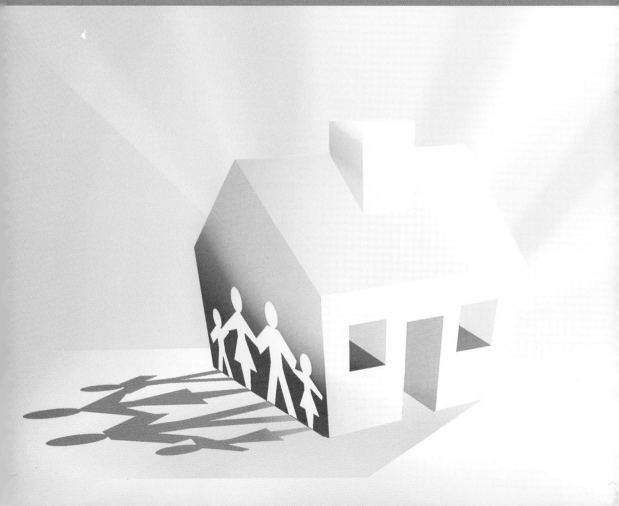

Philip Allan Updates, part of the Hodder Education Group, an Hachette Livre UK company, Market Place, Deddington, Oxfordshire OX15 0SE

Orders
Bookpoint Ltd, 130 Milton Park, Abingdon, Oxfordshire OX14 4SB
tel: 01235 827720
fax: 01235 400454
e-mail: uk.orders@bookpoint.co.uk
Lines are open 9.00 a.m.–5.00 p.m., Monday to Saturday, with a 24-hour message answering service. You can also order through the Philip Allan Updates website: www.philipallan.co.uk

ISBN 978-1-84489-638-7

First printed 2007
Impression number 5 4 3 2 1
Year 2012 2011 2010 2009 2008 2007

Printed in Spain

Philip Allan Updates' policy is to use papers that are natural, renewable and recyclable products and made from wood grown in sustainable forests. The logging and manufacturing processes are expected to conform to the environmental regulations of the country of origin.

P00983

Contents

Introduction

'I blame the family' is an expression commonly heard when antisocial behaviour is reported. Sociologists would agree that the family has an immense influence on individuals and society, though they disagree about almost everything else, including what a family is. This book helps you consider the dramatically conflicting perspectives and proposals for improving families, illustrated by examples from recent news. In the postmodern era, discussing only the UK family would be ethnocentric, so I have referred to alternative households in many parts of the world.

Chapter 1 explores definitions of the family, discusses whether nuclear families are universal and debates whether family life is beneficial to members or 'the source of all our discontents'. Chapters 2 and 3 provide further critical views of the family from a range of feminist and Marxist viewpoints.

Historical developments are the subject of Chapter 4, first focusing on how UK families adapted to industrialisation and then moving on to a contemporary scenario — the effects of globalisation on households in developing countries.

Chapters 5 and 6 examine family diversity, discussing the reasons for and the effects of, increased divorce, cohabitation and births outside marriage, and consider the influence of recent laws and social policies, for example allowing civil partnerships.

The final chapter looks at the controversial area of gender roles and power within the family, and whether the lives of children have changed for the better.

While reading the chapters in numerical order is recommended, there is a glossary to enable you to look up explanations that you may have bypassed. Tasks are included for you to think about as you work through the book, together with examination style questions with helpful guidance. These will provide practice in demonstrating the skills required by examiners to meet Assessment Objective 1 (AO1), clear communication of good knowledge and understanding, and Assessment ·Objective 2 (AO2), identification, analysis, interpretation and evaluation. There are ideas for practical research, references to websites and suggestions for further reading.

I hope you find this topic as fascinating as I do.

Jill Swale

What is a family, and how does it function?

The article contained in Box 1.1 reflects the common view of the family as the site of vital socialisation. It suggests the importance of caring adults as an influence on young people, and connects lack of such guidance with deviant lifestyles and poor life chances. While some sociologists would challenge aspects of the article, none would disagree that the families and alternative household arrangements in which people live are of considerable significance to those who want to understand society.

Box 1.1

UK teens 'worst in Europe'

Britain's youths are some of the worst behaved in Europe, according to new research. Studies by the Institute for Public Policy Research show British 15-year-olds are drunk more often, are involved in more fights and a higher proportion have had sex, compared with their counterparts in Germany, France and Italy.

The studies suggest that British adolescents can be defined by how they spend their spare time. While 45% of 15-year-old boys in England and 59% in Scotland spend most evenings with friends, in France that figure stands at just 17%.

In Europe, teenagers are more likely to sit down to a meal with their parents. In Italy, 93% eat regularly with their families, compared with 64% in the UK.

Nick Pearce, director of the IPPR, said the figures pointed to 'increasing disconnect' between children and adults, with youngsters learning how to behave from each other. 'Because they don't have that structured interaction with adults, it damages their life chances. They are not learning how to behave — how to get on in life — as they need to.'

Adapted from an article by Ali Martin in the *Sun* (2 November 2006)

Adults raised in a family can trace some interests, skills or attributes back to those with whom they grew up. In most cases, the standard of living of someone's family of origin has a profound effect on his or her opportunities and subsequent lifestyle. Children who, usually because of some misfortune, lack continuity of care by biological or adoptive parents are generally expected to be psychologically damaged. These points illustrate the important influence the family has on every aspect of adult life. In *Sociology of Family Life* (2002), David Cheal observes: 'We want to know how families of different kinds, in different places, produce different outcomes.'

Not all sociologists accept the commonsense view that family life is nurturing for its members and contributes to society's stability. While functionalists maintain this stance, Marxists, feminists and some psychologists identify negative aspects of the family, and there is evidence that non-family arrangements can sometimes be supportive. These differences of opinion make the family topic controversial and fascinating. Even defining the family is a matter of debate.

How is the family defined?

The influential US functionalist G. P. Murdock studied 250 societies ranging from simple to industrialised. In *Social Structure* (1949), he concluded that some form of family, in spite of variations in structure, existed in all of them. He therefore assumed that this must be the most satisfactory way for humans to conduct their lives. He defined a family thus:

> …a social group characterised by common residence, economic cooperation and reproduction. It includes adults of both sexes, at least two of whom maintain a socially approved sexual relationship, and one or more children, own or adopted, of the sexually cohabiting adults. The family is to be distinguished from marriage, which is a complex of customs centring upon the relationship between a sexually associating pair of adults within the family…
>
> G. P. Murdock, *Social Structure* (1949)

Murdock identified three types of family organisation through his cross-cultural survey. He called the most basic the **nuclear family**, consisting typically of a married man and woman and their offspring.

Though this type of family predominates in the USA, in other parts of the world nuclear families are affiliated into larger groupings. **Polygamy** involves plural marriages; under **polygyny**, common in African and Islamic cultures, a man acts as husband and father in several nuclear families concurrently. The much more rare arrangement of **polyandry** occurred in the past in Tibet, Nepal, the Canadian Arctic and Sri Lanka. This could also be regarded as a more complex nuclear family, involving one woman living with several husbands, often brothers, and their children.

Another adaptation is the **extended family**, consisting of two or more nuclear families living under a single roof or in adjacent buildings. A common type is the patriarchal family, where an older man is head of a family consisting of his wife or wives, unmarried children and his married sons with their wives and children. Such arrangements are found in traditional communities where many hands are needed to run the family farm.

Murdock observed that the nuclear family is a universal human social grouping:

> It exists as a distinct and strongly functional group in every known society…Whatever larger familial forms may exist…the nuclear family is always recognisable and always has its distinctive and vital functions — sexual, economic, reproductive, and educational…
>
> G. P. Murdock, *Social Structure* (1949)

Is the family universal?

Nayar relationships

Other sociologists have disagreed with Murdock's definition of the family, suggesting the existence of viable relationships not fitting his description. In an article 'Is the Family Universal? — The Nayar Case' (1968), E. Kathleen Gough summarised a marriage arrangement found in Kerala, India in the eighteenth century. Nayar men spent part of each year away from their villages, fighting in neighbouring kingdoms or undergoing military training, leaving **matrilineal** groups of women and children (kin based on female lines of descent) in the care of the eldest male. Every few years a grand ceremony was held, at which girls aged from 7 to 12 years were ritually married to local men, selected on the advice of an astrologer. The 'tali-husband', so named after the gold ornament he tied round his wife's neck, spent 3 days secluded with her, and then she had no further obligations to him, except to observe death rituals for him.

After the ritual marriage, she was publicly regarded as an adult woman and known as *amma*, meaning 'mother'. Shortly before or after puberty, she could accept sexually motivated visits from an indefinite number of Nayar men, known as *sandbandham* husbands, so long as they were not of a lower caste. These might include the tali-husband, but he had no priority.

> A husband visited his wife after supper at night and left before breakfast next morning. He placed his weapons at the door of his wife's room, and if others came later they were free to sleep on the verandah…Either party to a union might terminate it at any time without formality. A passing guest recompensed a woman with a small cash gift at each visit. But a more regular husband from within the neighbourhood had certain customary obligations…small personal gifts to her at the three main festivals of the year…Most important, when a woman became pregnant, it was essential for one or more men of appropriate subcaste to acknowledge probable paternity. This they did by providing a fee of a cloth and some vegetables to the lower-caste midwife who attended the woman in childbirth. If no man of suitable caste would consent to make this gift, it was assumed that the woman had had relations with a man of lower caste or with a Christian or a Muslim. She must then be either expelled from her lineage and caste or killed by her matrilineal kinsmen.

…In no sense of the term did a man maintain his wife. Her food and regular clothing she obtained from her matrilineal group…Even when physiological paternity was known with reasonable certainty, the genitor had no economic, social, legal or ritual rights in, nor obligations to, his children after he had once paid the fees of their births. Their guardianship, care and discipline were entirely the concern of their matrilineal kinsfolk.

E. K. Gough, 'Is the Family Universal?' — The Nayar Case' in Bell, N. and Vogel, E. (eds) *A Modern Introduction to the Family* (1968)

Gough concluded that the Nayar were a highly unusual example, undermining Murdock's description of the supposedly universal nuclear family because fathers were excluded from residential and socialising units. The anomaly probably arose because it provided a better source of support and satisfaction for women and children than monogamous relations with frequently absent fathers engaged in potentially fatal activities. It shows that domestic arrangements tend to arise in response to particular social circumstances.

Task 1.1

(1) Consider Murdock's definition and suggested functions of the family. In modern western society, which groups often viewed as families do not fit one or more of the features listed?

(2) Could any of the exceptions you have thought of arise, as in the case of the Nayar, from the inability of men to be consistent breadwinners for their wives and children? What is the likely effect on household structure?

Single-parent families

The **matrifocal** (mother-headed) single-parent family frequently arises in poor communities as a result of male unemployment or under-employment. Some ethnic groups subject to job discrimination, such as Afro-Caribbean families in the UK, may choose **consensual unions** (living together) over marriage, as this is more flexible. A couple may cohabit while the man has work, but later he may move away in search of another job and the woman will eventually become involved with another partner. Such a relationship has traditionally been regarded as a broken family, with a poor outlook for the successful upbringing of children. However, an alternative view is that, in the economic situation described, temporary cohabitation is more functional than marriage, as the woman does not have to spend her life struggling to support not only her children but also an unemployed male. In communities where such households are common, female relatives and friends may offer regular help to single mothers.

Household arrangements reflect cultural and religious norms as well as economic realities. Although in the UK men of Bangladeshi and Pakistani origin experience high unemployment, among those ethnic groups single-parent families are rare. The *izzat* or honour of women tends to be closely guarded so that cohabitation is unacceptable.

Among the white working class, on the other hand, where secular values predominate, the increasing shortage of unskilled manual jobs makes un-qualified young men, who are unlikely to become breadwinners, unattractive as marriage partners. The mothers of their children may prefer to live alone with their babies or to continue living with their natal family. Neither of these increasingly common arrangements fits Murdock's definition of economically cooperative adults of both sexes living with their children under the same roof.

The kibbutz

In an article 'Is the Family Universal? — The Israeli Case', Melford Spiro discusses the attributes of the **kibbutz**, 'an agricultural collective in Israel whose main features include communal living, collective ownership of all property…and the communal rearing of children'.

The kibbutz movement was based on socialist ideals. Kibbutzim vary in the details of how they are run, and nowadays young children may spend more time with their parents and sometimes live in the same rooms. In contrast, the extract below reflects the kibbutzim studied by Spiro in 1951–52, describing the more traditional type:

A kibbutz couple lives in a single room, which serves as a combined bedroom-living room. Their meals are eaten in a communal dining room, and their children are reared in a communal children's dormitory…Each mate works in some branch of the kibbutz economy, and each, as a member (chaver) of the kibbutz, receives his equal share of the goods and services that the kibbutz distributes. Neither, however, engages in economic activities that are exclusively directed to the satisfaction of the needs of his mate. Women cook, sew and launder…for the entire kibbutz… Men produce goods, but the economic returns for their labour go to the kibbutz, not to their mates…The education and socialisation of kibbutz children are the function of their nurses and teachers, and not of their parents. The infant is placed in the infants' house upon the mother's return from the hospital, where it remains in the care of nurses. Both parents see the infant there; the mother when she feeds it, the father upon return from work. The infant is not taken to its parents' room till its sixth month, after which it stays with them for an hour. As the child grows older, the amount of time he spends with his parents increases…though he must return to his children's house before lights-out.'

M. Spiro, 'Is the Family Universal? — The Israeli Case', in Bell, N. and Vogel, E. (eds) *A Modern Introduction to the Family* (1968)

Spiro initially concluded that kibbutz arrangements contradicted Murdock's definition of the family in almost every possible way. Later he revised his views. His thoughts are summarised in Table 1.1 on page 10.

Task 1.2

Consider which aspects of Murdock's description of the family would and would not apply in the following cases:

(1) A father spends most of the year away from his wife and child serving in the armed forces.

(2) Children are sent to boarding school.

(3) A gay couple live together and adopt a child.

(4) A couple with children divorce. The mother lives with a new male partner, her children and his children from a former relationship (a reconstituted family).

(5) Two brothers never marry and continue to live and work together at their original home, a farm, outliving their parents.

(6) Adults of both sexes, a few with children, joined Heaven's Gate religious cult, cutting themselves off from their former lives and moving to a remote location in the USA. Couples who arrived together renounced their sexual relationships and some agreed to castration. They lived fully as a community, eating all meals together and performing tasks assigned to them. They accepted the rulings of the cult's father figure in every aspect of daily living and eventually committed suicide together at his command.

Table 1.1 Spiro's thoughts on the extent to which a kibbutz resembles a family

Aspects of Murdock's family definition	Kibbutz unlike a family	Kibbutz like a family
Common residence	Children live in a separate house away from their parents.	Children visit parents' rooms for about 2 hours per evening. Adults spend more time with their own children than with other people's.
Economic cooperation and division of labour	There are no housewives or full-time mothers, and men are not breadwinners for their own partners and children. All adults work to support the whole community.	Adults' work contributes to the welfare of their own children and spouse. Work roles tend to be gendered, with women doing cooking and laundering for all.

Aspects of Murdock's family definition	Kibbutz unlike a family	Kibbutz like a family
Reproduction and socially approved relationship	Sexual relations are accepted between single people of over school age, and couples can request to share a room without being married. Women who marry retain their original name and status. All children are referred to as 'our children' by community members.	The granting of a room is based on the expectation of a more or less permanent and exclusive heterosexual union. Couples are expected to marry after, if not before, the birth of a child to give it legal rights according to state law. The children and their parents identify each other with conventional words such as 'mother' and 'son' and call their intimate group a *mishpacha* (family). Children of the kibbutz tend to marry outsiders (exogamy), as they regard the children they have grown up with as siblings, as if the entire community were a single family.
Socialisation and education of children	Most socialisation is done by nurses and teachers.	Parents assume the ultimate responsibility for their children's socialisation by ensuring that staff rear them according to acceptable guidelines.

Spiro's work suggests that it might be possible to accept Murdock's definition by regarding the whole kibbutz as one family. Alternatively, Murdock's view that the family is universal may need adjusting.

Clearly, Murdock's definition does not fit several arrangements commonly regarded as families, such as single-parent families, reconstituted families and civil partnerships with children. His term 'socially approved' is also problematic, as he clearly had marriage in mind, but these days cohabiting couples with children are increasingly common and generally accepted (though not necessarily 'approved' by all).

Other groupings of people not biologically related but sharing a house and economically cooperating, such as students, young singles, childless couples or small religious communities, are usually known as households. The term can include families and is also applied to the increasing proportion of people living alone.

How have functionalists viewed the family?

G. P. Murdock

As a functionalist, Murdock viewed society as a body where each part has a different role to play, contributing to the efficient operation of the whole organism. Institutions such as the family play a role in maintaining the social system, for example by producing law-abiding citizens and healthy, efficient workers. In addition, the distinctive roles played by family members complement each other so that each individual benefits. In *Social Structure* (1949), Murdock explained the four vital family functions:

- regulation of sexual activity
- production of new generations
- provision of economic support and the necessities of life through the division of labour
- socialisation of children into the culture of the community

Regulation of sexual activity

Sexual drive could lead to frequent conflict over partners, as in the animal kingdom, unless there are accepted rules. These include taboos against incest, which increases the risk of unhealthy offspring. Cooperation is best achieved by couples living together for the long term, and such a bond is cemented by a sexual union.

Production of new generations

Not only are couples residing together more likely to produce regular offspring, but mothers and babies are more likely to survive if fathers are at hand to protect and provide for them.

Provision of economic support and the necessities of life through the division of labour

Murdock observes:

By virtue of their primary sex differences, a man and a woman make an exceptionally efficient cooperating unit. Man, with his superior physical strength, can better undertake the strenuous tasks, such as lumbering, mining, quarrying, land clearance and house building. Not handicapped, as is the woman, by the physiological burdens of pregnancy and nursing, he can range farther afield to hunt, to fish, to herd and to trade. Woman is at no disadvantage, however, in the lighter tasks which can be performed in or near the home, e.g. the gathering of vegetable products, the fetching of water, the preparation of food, and the manufacture of clothing and utensils. All known human societies have developed specialisation and cooperation between the sexes roughly along this biologically determined line of cleavage...New tasks as they arise are assigned to one sphere of activities or to the other, in accordance with convenience and precedent.

G. P. Murdock, *Social Structure* (1949)

Socialisation of children into the culture of the community

The young human animal must acquire an immense amount of traditional knowledge and skill, and must learn to subject his inborn impulses to the many disciplines prescribed by his culture, before he can assume his place as an adult member of his society. The burden of education and socialization everywhere falls primarily upon the nuclear family...The father must participate as fully as the mother because, owing to the division of labour, he alone is capable of training the sons in the activities of adult males. Older siblings, too, play an important role.

G. P. Murdock, *Social Structure* (1949)

Task 1.3

(1) Feminists have been particularly sceptical of Murdock's reasons for the continuing existence of a gendered division of labour in contemporary societies. Think of several reasons why his explanation might be criticised.

(2) The majority of UK single-parent families are female-headed. If there is no father present to train sons in the activities of adult males, by what means might they learn how to be men?

Guidance (question 2)

Some New Right thinkers blame delinquency on fatherless boys copying unsuitable role models (see Chapters 5 and 6).

Evaluation of Murdock

Feminist Ann Oakley (1974) strongly disagreed with Murdock's view that all societies had similar gender roles and with the implication that these were inevitable and desirable. She re-examined his data, finding that he had ignored societies in which traditional gender roles were reversed or shared by both sexes. Tasmanian Aborigine women hunted, and Mbuti Pygmy parents shared responsibility for children. Margaret Mead's studies of New Guinea tribes (1935) revealed a similar variety of gender behaviour, the Tchambuli people reversing western expectations with female providers and decorative, gossiping men. Oakley therefore argued that the division of labour regarded as traditional in the west is not universal, and even one exception demonstrates that gender roles are socially constructed (created by society) rather than natural. In her opinion, the public male role carries higher status and is generally more interesting than the female domestic role, so western men have a vested interest in arguing against the possibility of change.

Furthermore, Murdock's examples about hunting and manufacture of clothing are irrelevant to advanced industrial societies. Relatively few tasks nowadays require physical strength and babies can be bottle fed, so there is no practical reason why a mother should not go out to work while her husband cares for their offspring. While it makes sense for a couple to divide duties between them, the particular division Murdock suggested reflected the contemporary US norm, with little acknowledgement of other possibilities.

Talcott Parsons

Talcott Parsons (1955) focused on the functions of the 'modern isolated' nuclear family in the USA. He acknowledged that many tasks and activities traditionally carried out within the kinship unit, such as making clothing, growing food and teaching children trades, were now performed by outside agencies such as businesses and colleges. This process of differentiation has left the family as a more specialised agency than before.

Increased divorce has been interpreted by some as evidence of family dis-organisation and decline, but Parsons viewed it as a response to the additional strain and responsibilities put on the parents of nuclear families, as they now live in greater isolation from wider kin and the community than in previous times. The family has increased in importance and carries out vital functions.

> It is because the human personality is not 'born' but must be 'made' through the socialization process that in the first instance families are necessary.
> T. Parsons and R. Bales, *Family, Socialization and Interaction Process* (1955)

The two essential functions of the family are:
- the socialisation of children so that they can truly become members of their society by internalising its culture
- the stabilisation of the adult personalities; living with children enables adults to express in a limited way the 'childish' elements of their own personalities, as well as the couple gaining emotional support from each other

Parsons discussed the reasons for differentiated sex roles within the family. If small groups have more than one leader, they adopt different roles for efficiency, but he asked why in the family women adopt the expressive (caring and nurturing) role whereas men take the instrumental role, as breadwinners and practical decision-makers. He suggested the answer lay:

...in the fact that the bearing and early nursing of children establish a strong presumptive primacy of the relation of mother to small child and this in turn establishes a presumption that the man, who is exempted from these biological functions, should specialise in the alternative instrumental direction.

T. Parsons and R. Bales, *Family, Socialization and Interaction Process* (1955)

Parsons suggested these biological orientations have been accentuated rather than weakened in the modern nuclear family. The isolation from kin means there are no other relatives to support the family financially, so the father *needs* to be the breadwinner. Mothers have to take greater responsibility for daily childcare than in an extended family arrangement and children are more emotionally dependent on their mother. Additionally, in Parsons's opinion, the modern-day expectation of romantic love within marriage encourages partners to emphasise rather than underplay their gender differences.

Parsons suggested that differentiation also occurs in children's family roles, as they differ from their parents in power and are brought up to be either expressive or instrumental, depending on their sex.

Table 1.2 Differentiation in family roles according to Parsons

Priorities	Instrumental	Expressive
Superior power	Father Technical expert Instrumental Executive leader	Mother Cultural expert Expressive Charismatic leader
Inferior power	Son Adequate technical performer Cooperator	Daughter Willing and accommodating person Loyal member

Adapted from figures 3 and 4 in T. Parsons and R. Bales, *Family, Socialization and Interaction Process* (1955)

Task 1.4

Consider Parsons's description of gender roles of adults and children within the family. Bear in mind that the source was American and written in 1955 by men.

- To what extent has the feminist movement of the late 1960s and 1970s changed our views about such matters?
- Has there been any change in the relative power of children and adults?
- To what extent has the view of the male as 'technical expert' disappeared in the UK?

Critics, particularly feminists, accused Parsons of complacency in his description of differentiated family roles. Despite acknowledging increasing divorce rates, he ignored the fact that, though efficient, the arrangements he described were not necessarily satisfying, especially for housewives.

Ronald Fletcher

Ronald Fletcher was a UK functionalist who painted an optimistic picture of the family and its functions. In *The Family and Marriage in Britain* (revised 1966) he disagreed with any suggestion that the family had lost its functions. His 'march of progress' theory suggests that, freed from the struggle for survival by the welfare state's economic safety net and basic services, the family can now concentrate on the 'essential' functions of caring for its members' emotional and sexual needs. It socialises the young, providing a stable home and a 'warm bath' to soak away the stresses of the outside world. Increased divorce shows that people now have high expectations of personal relationships and continue to seek better ones, whereas in the past many had to tolerate empty-shell marriages and might even live apart yet be unable to divorce.

> The bonds of love, affection and mutually accepted duties are the bonds on which marriage should rest, not the bonds of legal compulsion.
> R. Fletcher, *The Family and Marriage in Britain* (1966)

Fletcher wrote before the Divorce Reform Act of 1971, which produced a dramatic rise in the divorce rate, and before the women's movement drew public attention to the gender identity of the partner likely to be soaking in the 'warm bath'. Nevertheless, he anticipated other problems:

> The family is in danger of becoming too enclosed a group; there may be a danger in the more comfortable conditions of our society for people to become content with the garden, the warm fireside, the do-it-yourself kits, and, of course, the television screen.
> R. Fletcher, *The Family and Marriage in Britain* (1966)

Though the details now sound old fashioned, Fletcher was expressing a fear that lives were becoming too privatised.

> If we are concerned to improve the family and marriage, we cannot do this by concentrating on the family alone, but only by concerning ourselves with the attainment of social justice and improvements in human relationships throughout the whole of our society: in factories, schools, government and all other institutions.
> R. Fletcher, *The Family and Marriage in Britain* (1966)

Fletcher went on to describe the need to seek social justice worldwide, through organisations such as the United Nations. He suggested that by establishing a universal 'new family of man' through cooperation with others, individuals could better enjoy a fulfilling family life as well. His writing shows the danger of trying to 'pigeonhole' sociologists, as the view that privatised family life prevents people from engaging with social problems is more often associated with Marxists.

Shirley Zimmerman

A more recent view from Zimmerman (1988) is that families assume responsibility for some of the following functions:

- physical maintenance and care of group members
- addition of new members through procreation or adoption
- socialisation of children
- production, distribution and consumption of goods and services
- maintenance of motivation and morale through love

Why are families sometimes dysfunctional?

Task 1.5

Read the passage below and then consider the questions that follow.

Kids' stuff

What do you do when kids just won't listen? Camila Batmanghelidjh started listening to them instead. Kids Company is what the children of south London told her they needed.

Kids Company is a school, canteen and youth club visited by over 500 children a week, set up specifically for the most vulnerable children on London's streets. Many of the young people have dropped out of school; often they're homeless. The charity helps them regain access to care and education. But the unique thing about Kids Company is the attitude of its founder, whose refusal to be intimidated by the harsh circumstances of these kids' situations has allowed her to communicate with them where others have failed.

'I joke with the 17-year-old who's presenting himself as the biggest thug in Peckham, carrying his knife in his shoe. I think with a bit of love, a bit of humour and a bit of parenting we got through.'

TopFoto

The founder of Kids Company, Camila Batmanghelidjh

Task 1.5 (continued)

Something all the children share is a lack of parental care. 'On top of that they're badly traumatised by social circumstances: the exposure to violence is very high, there's a shooting every week. Many children tell me it's amazing they have survived. They cannot imagine themselves in the future.'

Kids Company endeavours to attract the children everybody else seeks to avoid, kids who don't belong anywhere. In the daytime, children not in school come for counselling and education. When the schools close at 4 p.m. the centre becomes a youth club, providing art classes, sport, music, books, hot food and an alternative to the streets. On Christmas Day over 150 children with no better offers filled the centre's gym for dinner, and Camila ensured there were presents for everyone.

Today she runs the charity through her belief in the 'healing powers of robust compassion and gentleness', helping children develop the ability to have respectful relationships.

Adapted from *Guardian Unlimited*, 2006
www.guardian.co.uk/prius/parttwo/story/0,,1214917,00.html

Does the passage suggest that:
- families are unnecessary, since institutions such as Kids Company provide a substitute?
- the family is so essential to our wellbeing that those not brought up in families become feral (lacking any sense of social responsibility)?
- modern families are dysfunctional, producing children like these?

The image of the close, loving family in Fletcher's study has been questioned by several social scientists and psychiatrists, who have described the western nuclear family as dysfunctional, both for its members and for society.

Are children mentally damaged by their families?

In his article 'The middle-class male child and neurosis' (*American Sociological Review*, xi, February 1946), Arnold Green found the turbulent family life of Catholic Polish immigrants, who frequently beat their numerous children and showed them little love, produced less mental illness in the young than the gentler upbringing of white, Protestant, middle-class Americans. The generation gap between Polish-speaking parents and their Americanised children meant that the children failed to identify with their parents and, though this resulted in little affection, there was little guilt either and the children assumed early independence. In contrast, the small Protestant family with college-educated parents was characterised by 'the physical and emotional blanketing of the child, bringing about a slavish dependence on the parents'.

Protestant parents had mixed feelings about deciding to have a child, as the expense of child-rearing depressed their standard of living, interrupted the wife's career and limited their intimacy. The mothers spent their days obsessively comparing their children's progress with others', while trying to prevent them from damaging the prized home.

In return for their efforts on their children's behalf, the parents expected their gratitude and when they offended them with disobedience, the parents threatened to withdraw their love. In the isolated family with few siblings, children were emotionally dependent on the parents and developed extreme guilt feelings that prevented them from asserting themselves in ways that might displease the parents. While love-withdrawal remained the mother's technique for controlling children at home, the father expressed disapproval when they failed to achieve in competitive situations in the outside world.

> But effective competition demands a certain amount of independence, firmness of purpose, perhaps aggressiveness…He is expected to 'do things', to accomplish, perhaps to lead in some endeavour…but his early social conditioning was dependence, submission, inferiority…An integrating of these conflicting roles is impossible. His conception of himself becomes one of abject failure.
>
> Arnold Green, 'The middle-class male child and neurosis' (1946)

Thus Green explained the mental illness frequently found in middle-class males. He suggested it was sometimes exacerbated by the Oedipus complex identified by Freud: a boy's hostility towards his demanding father, accompanied by guilt at such feelings, and an intensely close relationship with his loving mother that made relationships with females of his own age difficult to sustain.

Task 1.6

Read more about the work of psychiatrist Sigmund Freud (1856–1939), who argued that most mental illnesses in adults stem from inappropriate upbringing in the family. Useful sources are:

- http://en.wikipedia.org/wiki/Sigmund_Freud
- Davenport, G. (1991) *An Introduction to Child Development*, Collins Educational.
- Muncie, J. et al (eds) (1997) *Understanding the Family*, Open University.

Explore similar views expressed through twentieth-century novels such as D. H. Lawrence's *Sons and Lovers* and Philip Roth's *Portnoy's Complaint.* In both, the personalities of children are blighted by disproportionate guilt arising from oppressive parenting.

In the mid-1950s, Ezra Vogel and Norman Bell's influential study compared a group of US families, each with an emotionally disturbed child, with a matched group of 'well' families. This study is summarised in 'The emotionally disturbed child as the family scapegoat' (in Bell, N. and Vogel, E. (eds) (1968) *A Modern Introduction to the Family*, Free Press).

Vogel and Bell observed that parents often experience tensions as a result of conflicting values arising from their different backgrounds, career difficulties or failure to be accepted in a new neighbourhood. To express their hostility towards each other openly would lead to an angry confrontation, and perhaps marital break-up. Instead they focus their attention on one of their children, usually selecting one who mirrors some aspect of their own failure, such as the least attractive, the child making the slowest academic progress or a bed wetter. From then on, the parents view their problems as caused by the child, and even, unconsciously, encourage the child to become more deviant to give themselves further reasons to blame him or her. Thus, the scapegoat child receives no help to alleviate his or her problems, carries a burden of guilt for apparently causing the family's problems and becomes increasingly disturbed. Meanwhile, the parents are able to sustain their own relationship and usually maintain positions as steady workers. However, behaviour tolerated at home is deemed unacceptable in public, and the child's school, neighbours or relatives may insist on the child being diagnosed and receiving psychiatric treatment.

> In short, the scapegoating mechanism is functional for the family as a group but dysfunctional for the emotional health of the child and for his adjustment outside the family of orientation.
>
> N. Bell and E. Vogel, 'The emotionally disturbed child as the family scapegoat' (1968)

Likewise R. D. Laing, a radical psychiatrist, suggested with A. Esterson in *Sanity, Madness and the Family* (1964) that the nuclear family's members may make such conflicting demands upon each other that the more vulnerable sometimes become mentally ill. Schizophrenia may act as an escape route from an impossible situation. Laing was not value-free, since he belonged to a movement that put personal freedom above authoritative institutions like the family. Other psychiatrists believe that schizophrenia has physical as well as environmental causes.

Does the family damage wider social relationships?

In the 1967 Reith Lecture *A Runaway World?*, Edmund Leach argued that the modern nuclear family is so isolated and claustrophobic that its members expect too much of each other and explosions occur: 'The parents fight: the children rebel.' Moreover, the privatised nature of family life inculcates distrust of those who are different:

> The violence in the world comes about because we human beings are forever creating barriers between men who are like us and men who are not like us…Far from being the basis of the good society, the family, with its narrow privacy and tawdry secrets, is the source of all our discontents.
>
> Edmund Leach, Reith Lecture *A Runaway World?* (1967)

Marxists, such as David Cooper (1972), took a similar line, arguing that conformity to parental authority leads to mindless obedience at school and in the capitalist workplace. Child abuse and domestic violence have also been cited as evidence that the modern family is dysfunctional, and feminists have their own criticisms to add.

In defence of the family

More traditional thinkers, such as the Chief Rabbi Jonathan Sacks, continue to believe that family is a central institution for generating responsible behaviour and personal fulfilment:

> Watch a parent caring for a handicapped child. See a spouse coping with a partner suffering from Alzheimer's disease. Watch a family playing together in a park on a sunny afternoon, or a toddler taking its first steps and falling laughingly into outstretched parental arms. There is a beauty, undemonstrative, unselfconscious, that lives in a thousand small gestures of listening, caring, helping, giving, for no ulterior motive other than the fact that here we are 'we' not 'I'.
>
> The family is where passion, affection and companionship meet in the most intimate of human bondings. It is where, if we are blessed, we become most like God himself, bringing new life into the world through and for the sake of love. It is our first school, a miniature welfare state, a healthcare centre, a tutorial in responsibility. And yes, there is something spiritual about it. It is solitude redeemed.
>
> J. Sacks, 'The family is where we find passion, affection and companionship',
> *The Times* (15 May 2004)

Summary

- Sociologists study the family because of its influence on its members and society.
- Functionalist G. P. Murdock argued that some form of family (nuclear or extended) exists in all societies. It must therefore be the most satisfactory way to live.

- Critics have suggested that arrangements such as the matrifocal family and kibbutz undermine Murdock's description of the universal family.
- Other groupings of people, often not biologically related but sharing a house and resources, are known as households, as are the increasing proportion of people living alone.
- Murdock identified four functions of the family, while Parsons reduced these to two: the socialisation of children and stabilisation of adult personalities. Feminists have challenged the desirability of the expressive role for females and instrumental role for males.
- Fletcher argued that family life has improved in quality and is a source of fulfilment, despite increased divorce.
- Psychiatric studies have identified mental problems stemming from family relationships. Privatised family life may discourage people from relating well to non-family members.
- Religious leaders and other traditionalists continue to value the family.

Task 1.7

Examine the different functions performed by families for individual members and for society. (20 marks)

Guidance

- This is a typical examination question. Its main focus is on knowledge and understanding (AO1), so you need to provide plenty of detail from the work of Murdock, Parsons, Fletcher and Zimmerman, pointing out differences in emphasis and using their key vocabulary.
- Distinguish between services for individual members, such as feeding and comforting, and functions that impact on wider society, such as the production and socialisation of new generations of workers.
- You do not have to confine your knowledge to the western family but could discuss how functions vary between societies. There is interesting material about the Palestinian family in Cheal's *Sociology of Family Life*.
- Though the question does not explicitly ask you to assess functionalist views, evaluation (AO2) is expected in essays of this length. You could question the work of particular functionalists, and refer to views that families are sometimes dysfunctional for particular members and for society, drawing on the views of psychiatrists mentioned in this chapter and Marxists and feminists from Chapter 2.

Useful websites and videos

- Chief Rabbi Professor Jonathan Sacks: 'The family is where we find passion, affection and companionship'
  www.chiefrabbi.org/articles/credo/may04.htm
- Barton Peveril College Sociology Department
  http://home.barton.ac.uk/curriculum/humanities/sociology/index.htm
  Go to AS Index and click on Family Resources Index, then click on Functionalist View of Family
- Wikipedia article on polyandry; follow the links to other types of marriage
  http://en.wikipedia.org/wiki/Polyandry
- The Family (HaloVine videos)

Further reading

- Cheal, D. (2002) *Sociology of Family Life*, Palgrave.
- Jorgensen, N. (1995) *Investigating Families and Households*, Collins Educational.

How do feminists view the family?

How do feminist views on the family differ from those of functionalists?

> 'I'm just his wife and I've got a baby, and I'm not a person. I think that women definitely get taken for granted.'
>
> *The Ann Oakley Reader: Gender, Women and Social Science* (2005)

This was a typical response to feminist researcher Ann Oakley when she posed the question, 'Since you became a mother, have your views about the position of women changed at all?'

Functionalists assume that the family operates for the benefit of most members of society. Feminists disagree, highlighting women's exploitation as unpaid domestic workers and carers and their representation as limited individuals who can contribute little to public life. They also catalogue more dramatic forms of abuse.

The traditional view of gender roles held by Murdock and Parsons was that the division of labour between men as breadwinners and women as housewives and carers is the most efficient way of organising family life. As females are confined to the home during late pregnancy and breastfeeding, it is more practical for them to continue the caring role and for males to maintain their careers than for couples frequently to exchange roles.

Are gender differences innate?

Sociobiologists, such as David Barash (1979), go further, suggesting that contrasting male and female temperaments have evolved from biological traits. Women can usually only produce one baby a year and are certain it is theirs, so they are prepared to devote themselves to childcare and domesticity. Men, in contrast, can father children every day, without being sure babies are theirs, so they are more promiscuous and less caring towards children. Because they once needed to hunt for food for themselves, pregnant women and children, they developed aggression. This trait also enabled them to compete against other men for females, who are much more selective about their sexual partners, as they will be dependent on them during late pregnancy and lactation.

Task 2.1

Discuss to what extent you find Barash's explanation for the evolution of gentle women and assertive men relevant to gender roles in contemporary society.

Guidance

* Consider whether the temperaments Barash describes are still typical.
* As Barash's explanation is an evolutionary one, and there have recently been changes in reproductive technology, what are the implications for future gender roles?

Cultural representation of the sexes

Feminist Sherry Ortner (1974) noted the universal tendency for women to be associated with nature and men with culture in mythology, art, religious symbolism and literature. 'Nature' relates to childbirth, physical and emotional support of dependents, food preparation, sensitivity and intuition. In contrast, 'culture' requires a rational and assertive approach, referring to intellectual and creative activities, paid work, religious and political leadership and other aspects of public life. As we distinguish ourselves from the animal kingdom through our capacity to reason, culture carries far more status than nature, reflecting the progress of our civilisation.

Ortner implies that it is in the interests of men worldwide to continue portraying women as little different from animals and therefore incapable of rational action. Male control of the media and major religions allows the perpetuation of negative stereotypes of women, so patriarchy (dominance of society by older males) is preserved against potential female competition. Suggesting that the prevailing gender attributes are innate (present at birth) will discourage women from seeking new roles, as this appears to be going against nature. This is why feminists oppose sociobiologists, arguing instead that gender roles are socially constructed and therefore amenable to change.

Gender socialisation

Ann Oakley in an early study, *Housewife* (1974), suggested that children learn gender roles very early within the family. Society's assumptions about how the sexes should behave are reinforced by 'canalisation'. Parents direct children into gender-appropriate activities through choice of toys, activities and dress, and comments that shape particular self-images, such as 'That's a brave boy', 'What a pretty girl'.

Angela McRobbie's study of working-class girls (1975) showed they had absorbed the ideology of romance, the view that their only options in life were marriage and children. Study and careers came low in their priorities, and female teenagers spent their leisure time practising makeup and hairstyles ready for courtship, while boys played in the street. Sue Sharpe's interviews for *Just Like a Girl: How Girls Learn to be Women* (1976) produced similar findings, but her interviews with similar girls for the 1994 edition showed that teenage girls had become more ambitious. In response to changes in society, they realised the importance of education and financial independence, while marriage and having children were lower priorities. This recent awareness is attributable to the influence of the feminist movement of the 1960s and 1970s, known as second wave feminism to distinguish it from nineteenth-century campaigns for married women's property rights and the vote. It focused on raising consciousness, and made reluctant housewives realise their exploitation was a widespread phenomenon that could be challenged.

How significant was second wave feminism?

The Feminine Mystique

Betty Friedan's book *The Feminine Mystique* (1963) explored the attitudes that perpetuated the gendered division of labour.

Betty Friedan

TopFoto

> The problem lay buried, unspoken, for many years in the minds of American women…. Each suburban wife struggled with it alone. As she made the beds, shopped for groceries, matched slipcover material, ate peanut butter sandwiches with her children, chauffeured Cub Scouts and Brownies, lay beside her husband at night, she was afraid to ask even of herself the silent question — 'Is this all?'
>
> Betty Friedan, *The Feminine Mystique* (1963)

Women's acceptance of their role was due to socialisation:

They learned that truly feminine women do not want careers, higher education, political rights…all they had to do was devote their lives from earliest girlhood to finding a husband and bearing children…In the fifteen years after World War II, this mystique of feminine fulfilment became the cherished and self-perpetuating core of contemporary American culture.

Betty Friedan, *The Feminine Mystique* (1963)

Friedan realised that unsatisfied women blamed themselves or their marriages, believing that 'words like "emancipation" and "career" sounded strange and embarrassing'.

What were the aims of liberal feminists?

By the 1960s, more American women were college educated and some became involved in the civil rights movement. This drew their attention to gendered (as well as racial) discrimination, and in 1966 many joined Betty Friedan to found the National Organisation of Women (NOW). They campaigned for maternity leave, childcare centres, equality in education and job training and the rights of women to control their reproductive lives.

Feminists who believe gender equality can be achieved by legislation and the gradual softening of attitudes through education and the media are known as **liberal feminists**. Friedan adopted this moderate approach, envisaging a future in which:

…men and women share not only children, home and garden, not only the fulfilment of their biological roles, but the responsibilities and passions of the work that creates the human future and the full knowledge of who they are.

Betty Friedan, *The Feminine Mystique* (1963)

Thus her vision of female emancipation retained the conventional family structure, differing only in affording women the chance to have stimulating careers and encouraging men to undertake caring roles and traditionally 'feminine' careers if they so wished.

Feminist ideas spread to the UK and western Europe, generating sociological studies. Oakley (1974) provided supporting data for the grievances, calculating that UK women spent an average of 77 hours a week on domestic duties. Although critics suggest her questions were loaded, many agree that housewives are frequently isolated, and bored by repetitive, unpaid chores. Jessie Bernard (1976) carried out a comparative study of single and married women, identifying in the latter wide-scale prevalence of the 'housewife syndrome' — the depression and symptoms of stress arising from the frustrations of housework.

Some women, instead of joining formal organisations such as NOW, preferred women's liberation groups. These were leaderless consciousness-raising gatherings that shared personal experiences and discussed the nature of men's power over women and how to eradicate it. Sometimes they examined gendered issues beyond the domestic sphere, such as the observation in Dale Spender's *Man Made Language* (1980) that the English language assumes people are male unless otherwise stated. A similar objection to the tendency of history to focus on male deeds ('his' story) led to the search for forgotten achievements of women, known as 'herstory'.

What were the aims of radical feminists?

Some women felt that legal changes alone would have little effect on female exploitation and that men could not be persuaded to relinquish their dominant position. Radical feminists believe that only drastic changes at the roots of society will help women.

In the influential text *Sexual Politics* (1970), Kate Millett drew parallels between leaders' rule over subjects and men's domination of women. She noted how society was a patriarchy, with every sphere controlled by men:

> The military, industry, technology, universities, science, political office, and finance — in short, every avenue of power within the society, including the coercive power of the police, is entirely in male hands...What lingers of supernatural authority, the Deity, 'His' ministry, together with the ethics and values, the philosophy and art of our culture, its very civilisation...is of male manufacture.
>
> Kate Millett, *Sexual Politics* (1970)

Males are socialised to be assertive, women to submit. This patriarchal ideology is 'interiorised', absorbed through religion, myth, sexist vocabulary and works of literature such as Mailer's *An American Dream*, in which the male protagonist strangles his wife then rapes the maid. Millett cited other authors such as Henry Miller and D. H. Lawrence, in whose works male sexual domination of women is glorified.

> Expectations the culture cherishes about his gender identity encourage the young male to develop aggressive impulses, and the female to thwart her own or turn them inward. The result is that the male tends to have aggression reinforced in his behaviour, often with significant anti-social possibilities.
>
> Kate Millett, *Sexual Politics* (1970)

She observed that the American phrase 'the guy has balls' approvingly links maleness with assertiveness, whereas passivity is reinforced in females. Fear of male violence, rape and abuse restricts women's activities so they avoid going out alone at night. Women who behave like men, abandoning such precautions, are likely to experience victim-blaming if their actions result in rape or attack.

Task 2.2

Which of the following examples of patriarchy cited by Millett are still prevalent in western societies today?

- Women having no legal standing, unable to keep their own earnings.
- Women not being paid for housework.
- Women lacking technological expertise so they cannot manage everyday life without men.
- Women gravitating towards the humanities and social sciences, resulting in poorer paid work than in the male-dominated areas of science, technology and business.
- Adulteresses being stoned to death, with no penalty imposed on male correspondents.
- Patriarchal legal systems depriving women of control over their bodies, driving some to die of illegal abortions.
- Pornographic media exploiting women.
- Wife beating.

Domestic violence, though frequently unreported, may be as widespread today as when *Sexual Politics* was written. The situation was recently summed up by Marsha Jones (2006):

> Each year, around 120 women are killed by their partners…Most of the women had experienced domestic violence for several years before they were killed. However what is surprising is that the sentences for these crimes were generally much shorter than for other such cases. Courts were referred to the woman's infidelity or her 'nagging'…
>
> In their latest study, Rebecca and Russell Dobash look at the backgrounds of men who murdered their partners. They claim that those who had previously used violence against women tended to have more 'conventional' backgrounds than men who murdered other men. They did not come from violent homes, nor had they been victims of domestic abuse, but they had used violence before and on previous partners — in a sense they specialised in domestic violence against women. Many of these domestic murders occurred at significant times — when the relationship was splitting up or after it had ended. As Dobash and Dobash say, 'The thread that runs through this is the man's sense of ownership of the woman and his control over the continuation of the relationship'.
>
> Marsha Jones, 'Synopsis: domestic violence', Sociology Review
(Vol. 16, No. 1, September 2006)

Millett (1970) observed that patriarchy has a 'powerful hold through its successful habit of passing itself off as nature'. The legislative changes negotiated by liberal feminists are unlikely to shift such deeply entrenched and universal male domination. Instead there is need for a 'sexual revolution'.

Shulamith Firestone argued along similar lines in *The Dialectic of Sex: The Case for Feminist Revolution* (1970), suggesting that women had to question 'even the very organisation of nature'. Women throughout history have been at the mercy of their biology, dependent on males during pregnancy, childbirth and infant care, resulting in a gendered division of labour and imbalance of power. Firestone recommended:

> …the freeing of women from the tyranny of their reproductive biology by every means available, and the diffusion of the childbearing and childrearing role to the society as a whole, men as well as women.
>
> Shulamith Firestone, *The Dialectic of Sex: The Case for Feminist Revolution* (1970)

Firestone maintained that married family living should be replaced by various options, including more people living as singles, couples not intending to have children cohabiting without legal ties, and households of ten or so consenting adults applying for a licence to live together for 7 to 10 years to raise children. The latter would be achieved artificially, using the test-tube baby method, so women would be spared the discomfort of pregnancy and childbirth and would be financially independent of men as they could work continuously. Particular adults would not be 'decreed "mother" and "father"', so they would not feel possessive about the children in their group; all the household adults and older children would care for each child for as long as necessary and 'no one person would ever be involuntarily stuck with it'.

Firestone argued that this system would generate intimate relationships between household adults and children based on spontaneous choice and perhaps resulting in life-long attachments, instead of uncaring parents neglecting 'their' children, as in the present system. Children would no longer be minors, so they could transfer out of an unsatisfactory household and, because sexuality was separate from childbirth, marriage and power relationships, there should be no taboos over sexual relationships between people of any age or either sex, allowing complete freedom of emotional expression.

Long compulsory schooling could be replaced by education in basic skills, supplemented by more specialist training at any time of life; this would enable adolescents to be financially independent as they could start paid work earlier than is presently the case.

The birth of children to a group of adults who might disband as soon as the children were old enough to be independent, would also eliminate class privilege based on birth, as family wealth would no longer be passed down. Thus not only would patriarchal power vanish as children and women would no longer be economically dependent on adult males, but capitalism would be undermined, as wealth and class attitudes would no longer be passed down the generations.

Task 2.3

Shulamith Firestone said of the abolition of the family described in *The Dialectic of Sex*: 'We now have the knowledge to create a paradise on earth anew.'
- Discuss possible advantages and problems of the new social arrangements Firestone suggested. Would it be 'paradise'?
- Compare Firestone's ideas with similar arrangements described in the novel *Brave New World* by Aldous Huxley (1932).

What have feminists achieved?

The Women's Liberation Movement gained much support during the 1970s, generating public attention and attitude change. Legislation benefiting women that could be attributed to feminist influence includes the following:
- Abortion Act 1967, allowing social (in addition to medical) grounds for terminating a pregnancy.
- Divorce Reform Act 1969, broadening grounds for divorce to include irretrievable breakdown of marriage.
- Equal Pay Act 1970, by which women had to be paid the same as men for the same job.
- Sex Discrimination Act 1975, relating to employment, education and advertising and establishing the Equal Opportunities Commission.
- Domestic Violence Act 1976, increasing protection for battered wives.
- Equal Value Amendment to Equal Pay Act 1984, allowing women to claim equal pay for jobs similar to those done by males.
- Outlawing of marital rape in 1994 as part of the Criminal Justice Act.

All of the above affected the nature of family life directly, or did so indirectly by encouraging more women to undertake paid work.

What is third wave feminism?

The mainstream feminist movement was followed by a series of smaller movements of groups of women whose specific grievances had not been addressed.

For example, Jewish feminists formed their own groups to discuss the polarisation in Orthodox circles between a woman's traditional responsibilities as keeper of a kosher home and a man's more public role in the synagogue. They particularly objected to the lack of female rites of passage ceremonies in Judaism, and some devised their own liturgies to be said at important times for women, such as at the onset of menstruation, the birth of female children and the menopause.

Eco-feminists, unlike most other feminists, argued that women were essentially different from men in temperament, being more peace loving and in tune with nature as a result of their experience of childbirth. They blamed men for the competitiveness that generates industrial pollution and war. Some of these groups met to engage in creative projects or feminist spirituality, exploring modern forms of witchcraft, nature worship and goddess movements. Some of the more radical eco-feminists set up all-female communes, preferring sisterhood to male oppression.

Other types of women, such as lesbians, disabled women and members of different religious and ethnic groups, have set up their own specific groups, a development known as third wave or difference feminism. Some of these are still very active, especially in the developing world.

Is feminism still relevant?

Some sociologists suggest western society has now entered a period of post-feminism, characterised by:

- loss of interest in feminism by most women, who complacently believe they have achieved equality
- disillusionment of some women, who feel that 'trying to have it all' is too stressful and a return to traditional domestic roles is more fulfilling
- campaigns to reassert men's rights apparently marginalised as a result of feminist demands (a position taken by the UK Men and Fathers' Rights Organisation)

However, though mainstream feminism is not as high profile as in the 1970s, feminist sociologists have continued to conduct research and generate ideas. Susan Faludi in *Backlash: the Undeclared War against Women* (1992) quoted from a wide variety of US media suggesting that feminism had made women less happy, citing burn-out, depression and childlessness of professional women as examples. She challenged this view, arguing that if women were unhappy it was because equal rights had not been achieved — for example, they still shouldered 70% of household duties.

> The 1980s saw a powerful counterassault on women's rights, a backlash, an attempt to retract a handful of small and hard won victories that the feminist movement did manage to win for women...We have seen New Right politicians condemn women's independence, anti-abortion protesters firebomb women's clinics, fundamentalist preachers damn feminists as 'whores' and 'witches'...Although the backlash is not an organised movement, that doesn't make it any less destructive...These whispers and threats and myths move overwhelmingly in one direction: they try to push women back into their 'acceptable roles' — whether as Daddy's girl or fluttery romantic, active nester or passive love object.
>
> Susan Faludi, *Backlash: the Undeclared War against Women* (1992)

Laura Purdy (1997) also expressed concern that even feminists had forgotten second wave critiques of the family and took it for granted that they should have children. She maintained that pronatalism should be condemned, as it persuades many women to have children they really do not want and cannot care for adequately. Patriarchal society provides little recognition of the burden of having children, especially the burden on poor and single women.

> How can women energetically fight the entrenched sexism in society and pursue positions of power and prestige if their time and energy is mostly taken up with children's needs?...Equality is doomed unless women temporarily refrain from child-rearing so that they can devote themselves to changing the situation...I suspect that this development would open women's eyes to the fact that society wants babies, but that it prefers women to think that producing them is both naturally women's lot and that doing so is an individual decision. After all, in those circumstances society owes women no help in bringing up new generations. If women stopped having babies, the resulting pressures would unmask this reality.
>
> Laura Purdy, 'Babystrike!' in *Feminism and Families* (ed. Hilde Lindemann Nelson) (1997)

Purdy concedes that some women would be reluctant to follow her advice, especially deprived women who viewed childbirth as their only outlet, though good social programmes might widen their horizons. Failing that, if the baby strike were only conducted by white middle-class women, it could be sufficient to influence the attitudes of powerful men. Purdy's article shows that radical ideas not very different from those proposed by Firestone in 1970 continue to be entertained, even in a supposedly post-feminist period.

How are women in developing countries oppressed?

Even those claiming that women in some developed countries now 'have it all' would not say the same for Asian, African and South American women.

The United Nations Population Fund reported in the year 2000 that:

- as many as 5,000 women are killed annually in so-called 'honour killings' (many for the dishonour of having been raped)
- an estimated 4 million women and girls are bought and sold worldwide each year into marriage, prostitution or slavery
- 130 million women worldwide have undergone female genital mutilation
- 20 million women each year undergo unsafe abortions
- across the world at least 1 in every 3 women has been beaten, coerced into sex or abused, usually by someone known to them

Cindi Katz and Janice Monk (1993) noted that in African and Asian countries, girls were less likely to receive secondary education than boys. The effect tends to be early and frequent pregnancies, resulting in babies with lower birth weight, compromising infant health and survival.

> Socially constructed life-course patterns, such as age of marriage and childbearing, have serious implications for health and education in general.
> J. Monk and C. Katz (eds) *Full Circles: Geographies on Women over the Life Course*
> (1993)

Male children are preferred in many parts of the world, receiving disproportionate amounts of food, healthcare, education and maternal attention. Where there are strict government controls over family size, excessive female mortality follows.

> Girls are being aborted, killed and neglected at staggering rates in several regions, and these practices are showing up increasingly in skewed population ratios. In India and China alone, conservative estimates point to over 52 million missing females.
> J. Monk and C. Katz (eds) *Full Circles: Geographies on Women over the Life Course*
> (1993)

Summary

- Feminists believe that women are disadvantaged within the family as unpaid domestic workers and carers. They disagree with the views that the traditional gendered division of labour is the most efficient or natural way to live, maintaining that gender roles and characteristics result from socialisation in patriarchal societies.
- Liberal feminists believe that attitudes, such as adherence to the feminine mystique, can be gradually changed and legislation can bring about gender equality.
- Radical feminists have drawn attention to extreme abuses of male power such as rape, domestic violence and pornography. Some believe women will

continue to be dominated by the husbands by whom they bear children and the only solution is to produce children outside the conventional family.

- While second wave feminists were predominantly white and middle class, difference feminists have focused on the specific needs of women from less advantaged backgrounds.
- Currently, attention is focused on the gross gender inequalities in developing countries.

Task 2.4

Examine ways in which feminist researchers have contributed to sociological understanding of family roles and relationships. (20 marks)

Guidance

- This is a typical examination question. The key word 'examine' indicates that the main focus is on knowledge and understanding (AO1), though some evaluation (AO2) marks are available for comparisons between different types of feminism and criticism of studies.
- Plan your essay carefully, as there is potentially a great deal of information to include. Ensure that you focus on feminists' contributions to sociological understanding rather than the legislative changes they have encouraged.
- Confine your comments to family issues; media representation and low pay are only relevant in so far as they impact on women's lack of power and independence within the family.
- Begin with a general definition of feminism. Then plan different sections on liberal, radical and difference feminism. Add in Marxist feminism after reading the next chapter. Ensure that you name several researchers for each section and use their key vocabulary such as 'patriarchy' to gain knowledge marks.
- Avoid simply listing researchers' views. Identify the particular points they have 'contributed to sociological understanding', and if you feel some of their ideas are impractical or no longer relevant briefly say why.
- Conclude the essay with some general comments about feminists' influence on the sociology of the family. This could involve identifying the most important contributions, in your opinion, and possible consideration of whether, in a supposedly 'post-feminist' period, they have a continuing role.

Research suggestion

Interview young women to see whether they hold 'post-feminist' attitudes. Do they believe women still need to strive for equality, are they complacent or do they believe that 'trying to have it all' is too stressful? Avoid asking leading questions.

Useful websites and videos

- Wikipedia article on feminism with leads to follow about different types
  http://en.wikipedia.org/wiki/Feminism
- Amnesty International site on women's human rights
  www.amnestyusa.org/women/violence/
- United Nations report 'The state of world population 2000' on men and women in a time of change
  www.unfpa.org/swp/2000/english/
- HaloVine videos interviewing Sue Sharpe on *Just Like a Girl* and Ann Oakley on *Housewife*

Further reading

- Nelson, H. (1997) *Feminism and Families*, Routledge.
- Oakley, A. (2005) *The Ann Oakley Reader: Gender, Women and Social Science*, Policy Press.

How have Marxists viewed the family?

> So long as capitalism exists, it is impossible for either women or men to gain full dignity and humanity, other than by fighting oppression. It is with that perspective that we try to win the best of the new generation of feminists to the Socialist Workers Party, to raise their consciousness to revolutionary socialist consciousness, and to organise and inspire the masses of women to fight to change society.
>
> *Feminism and Socialism* (ed. Linda Jenness) (1972)

The stirring speech above is part of a resolution entitled 'Towards a Mass Feminist Movement', passed at the 1971 National Convention of the Socialist Workers' Party in the USA. It was the first comprehensive document produced by the left-wing organisation that analysed women's oppression, showing how it was being influenced by the feminist movement. This chapter will begin by examining how traditional Marxists (often male) viewed the family, and then considers the influence of Marxist feminists, who showed greater concern for the rights of women alongside the need to liberate the working class as a whole.

How did traditional Marxists view the family?

Karl Marx (1818–83) deplored the way contemporary western societies were dominated by a wealthy and powerful class, the bourgeoisie. This class maintained control over the rest of society through ownership of the means of production (such as businesses), by employing the proletariat (working class) for low wages and by keeping the profits for its own members. Despite the potential for conflict in this unfair situation, the masses tended to accept this state of affairs as inevitable, natural or even sanctioned by God. They remained in this state of false consciousness as their views were influenced by capitalist ideology, which permeated all the institutions in society: the government, the media, religion, the education system and the family.

Modern Marxists continue to follow these basic ideas, even though western societies have become more democratic with welfare benefits for the needy. Controlling people through ideas rather than physical force is known as hegemony. By socialising the young to accept inequalities as normal, the family perpetuates class domination. Thus, unlike Murdock, Marxists regard the family's function to bring up children to abide by the norms of capitalist society and become cooperative workers as undesirable. Their desired objective is a communist society, in which all means of production (such as farms and factories) are collectively owned and workers receive a fair share of the profits, thus abolishing poverty. Marx called his own theory 'socialism', a term often used interchangeably with communism and sometimes used to mean a less radical attempt to redistribute resources more evenly.

Engels, linking the family with capitalism

Karl Marx's collaborator, Friedrich Engels, suggested that the exploitation of women in families started at the same time as capitalism. In *The Origin of the Family, Private Property and the State* (1902), he drew on anthropological evidence to suggest that natural, egalitarian relationships were replaced by monogamous marriage once people began to farm successfully enough to produce a surplus. Passing accumulated private property down the male line became the dominant practice, and marriage, by confining women's sexual activities, ensured supremacy of the man in the family.

Friedrich Engels

Women came to be regarded as dependents, whose main purpose was to produce legitimate heirs, and second to be domestic servants. They were expected to spend most of their time at home out of temptation's way, and codes of sexual morality punished a wife's infidelity more than her husband's.

Though Engels's theory is based on unreliable historical evidence, it neatly links women's exploitation with the pursuit of wealth. He asked whether there would be any need for marriage following 'the impend-ing social revolution', when private property would be owned communally.

TopFoto

Task 3.1

Read the passage by Engels and discuss the questions that follow.

> Only modern large-scale industry again threw open to her — and only to the proletarian woman at that — the avenue to social production: but in such a way that, when she fulfils her duties in the private service of her family, she remains excluded from public production and cannot earn anything: and when she wishes to take part in public industry and earn her living independently, she is not in a position to fulfil her family duties…Today, in the great majority of cases, the man has to be the earner, the breadwinner of the family, at least among the propertied classes, and this gives him a dominating position… In the family he is the bourgeois; the wife represents the proletariat… The first premise for the emancipation of women is the reintroduction of the entire female sex into public industry…This again demands that the specific feature of the individual family of being the economic unit of society be abolished.
>
> Friedrich Engels, *The Origin of the Family, Private Property and the State* (1902)

Explain why Engels felt that women's paid work is incompatible with the conventional family.

Do you agree with his view that women working in industry are in a better position than housewives?

The monogamous family would cease to be an economic unit; children, whether legitimate or not, could be cared for and educated by the state; and religion would be so weakened that there would be no pressure on couples who were no longer in love to stay together. He predicted a time when people could follow their feelings spontaneously, and no one would have to marry or stay married for economic security.

The family under Soviet Communism

Engels's ideas were extremely influential in the first few years after the Russian revolution of 1917. In an article entitled 'The fate of the family in Soviet Russia: 1917–44' (1968), H. Kent Geiger described the debate about whether people should be forced suddenly to give up 'bourgeois family living' or whether changes could be allowed to occur gradually. Communists believed that spending free time in the family home was too privatised, acting against the community spirit needed for people to work together in collective farms and public organisations. A moderate position was expressed by an influential member of the Leningrad Party organisation:

An openly negative attitude to the family under present conditions does not have sufficient grounding, because pre-socialist relationships still exist, the state is still weak, the new social forms [public dining rooms, state rearing of children and the like] are as yet little developed, and until then the family cannot be abolished completely. However, the coordination of this family with the general organization of Soviet life is the task of every Communist…One must not shut oneself off in the family, but rather grow out of the family shell in the springboard from which we must leap into the future.

Quoted from a Russian source (A. Slepkov, Moscow, 1926) by H. Kent Geiger in 'The fate of the family in Soviet Russia: 1917–44' in Bell, N. and Vogel, E. (eds) *A Modern Introduction to the Family* (1968)

The authorities' intention was that all women should be engaged in 'social production', and their traditional chores of child rearing, preparing food and washing clothes should be undertaken by state-run organisations, as in the kibbutz. Lenin argued that this would liberate women from drudgery and put them in touch with communist values. He maintained that it was women who lagged behind in their understanding of revolutionary ideals, like worms invisibly rotting the determination of their husbands. Maintaining individual households was not cost effective, and the time saved could be harnessed for centralised production for economic growth. Rearing children in communal houses connected by a gallery with the adult quarters would free mothers for work and accustom the young to collective living rather than outmoded private life. Gradually, terms such as 'my parents' and 'our children' would fall out of usage.

Geiger summarised the views of one of the more radical reformers, L. M. Sabsovich, who wanted a thorough cultural revolution:

This was to include complete separation of children from parents from the earliest years. Sabsovich argued that the child is the property of the state, not of the individual family. The state therefore has the right to compel parents to surrender their children to special 'children's towns' to be built 'at a distance from the family'… In the new city not only work but all aspects of leisure and consumption activities were to be organised on a collective basis. The family dwelling would be completely eliminated, to be replaced by individual rooms for individual persons. (Married persons would have adjoining rooms.)

H. Kent Geiger in 'The fate of the family in Soviet Russia: 1917–44' in Bell, N. and Vogel, E. (eds) *A Modern Introduction to the Family* (1968)

Even Lenin's widow opposed Sabsovich's ideas about children's towns, but less drastic changes came into law. Divorce became much easier and women were given equal rights with men. The state was unable to provide the planned public dining halls, nurseries and laundries in the post-revolutionary turmoil, so abortion was legalised in order to free women for work. Childless couples were not allowed to adopt, as this was viewed as encouraging traditional families.

The problems of these policies soon became apparent. The birth rate fell and men casually divorced wives without providing for their children, leaving mothers struggling with multiple responsibilities. There were insufficient state institutions to care for orphaned children, leading to vagrancy and delinquency. In 1934, Stalin turned the tide by denouncing divorce and sexual freedom, making abortion illegal and legitimising the family under a new name: the 'Soviet socialist family'. Propaganda recommended large families so that children could learn to subordinate their individual wishes to a greater good, with the family acting as a small collective in preparation for public life. By the 1940s, housework (described by Lenin as petty drudgery) was redefined as socially useful labour. Stable marriages and family responsibilities became more important to the regime than individual freedom, sexual equality and ideological consistency.

Task 3.2

Consider the change in attitude to the family in Soviet Russia between 1917 and 1944. How might functionalists use this material to support their views on the family?

Guidance

Consider the family functions identified by Murdock and the degree to which they were achieved when Soviets tried to dissolve the family.

Zaretsky: improving the family under socialism

US Marxist Eli Zaretsky censured radical lesbianism or separatism because it aimed at personal transformation, but left the rest of society unchanged, blaming patriarchy when it should be opposing capitalism. In *Capitalism, the Family and Personal Life* (1976), he criticised radical feminists such as Firestone for focusing on women's exploitation within the family, and for their proposals for all-female communes that attracted only a few middle-class white women and would not be sustainable. Zaretsky considered liberal feminists more effective, attracting larger numbers of women in their campaigns for equal pay and more childcare.

He praised Juliet Mitchell's *Woman's Estate* (1971) for applying Marxist thought to feminist questions. Mitchell noted that the family preserved capitalism by reproducing the labour force and by socialising children into valuing private property. Children grow up prepared to work hard under capitalism in order to buy consumer products to improve their own hard-won leisure. Though contraception reduced the burden of the large family, increasingly high expectations of childcare and home maintenance continued to oppress women. Even working women remained financially dependent on men because of career breaks while their children were young — years in which they might otherwise have been active in trade unions, pressing for better working conditions for women. Capitalist ideology claims the family is a site of individualism and freedom, yet in truth it involves 'the inculcated obedience of children, subservience of the wife' (Juliet Mitchell, *Woman's Estate*, 1971).

While agreeing with all this, Zaretsky viewed Mitchell's account as flawed by her suggestion that, while Marxists need to transform the economic base, the exploitation of women in the family could be addressed by changing gender attitudes through methods such as psychoanalysis. He criticised her for viewing the family and the world of paid work as separate spheres of oppression requiring different solutions.

Zaretsky linked changes in the family and personal life to economic developments:

- In the late Middle Ages, women worked alongside men in cottage industries and participated in many trade guilds.
- In the early days of the industrial revolution, lower-class men, women and children worked together in the new factories.
- However, legislation eventually restricted child labour so that mothers frequently looked after their children at home while men drew a 'family wage'.
- By the mid-nineteenth century, many women were cut off from paid labour and inhabited a separate sphere from men, their unpaid domestic labour valued less.
- In the early twentieth century, as automation made working hours shorter and jobs less interesting, alienated male workers looked to the private sphere of the family for relaxation and personal fulfilment. Women were assigned compassionate, nurturing roles towards husbands and children.
- Increased wages made the family a target for the consumption of rapidly obsolete goods promoted by advertising, adding to the pressure on women to maintain beautiful homes. Cheap house wares and fashions distracted workers from their frustration, increasing the sense that people's identity lay not in their work but in lifestyles pursued at home in leisure time. Thus personal life, including housework and child rearing, was viewed as a separate sphere from paid work.

Zaretsky criticised the US Communist party for focusing exclusively on the need to transform relations of workers and capitalists and for assuming that this would automatically bring beneficial changes to the family.

Every programme developed by socialists for female liberation depended on the entry of women into the wage labour force. Similarly feminists, before the emergence of the current women's movement, sought to liberate women through an emphasis on jobs, equal pay, education…through the ballot. The result, as in the Russian Revolution or in early twentieth century American feminism, has been to transform the position of women as wage labourers and professionals or in political life, while leaving women's place within the family relatively intact.

Eli Zaretsky, *Capitalism, the Family and Personal Life* (1976)

Zaretsky recommended:

- learning from the failures of Russian communism to plan more carefully for the liberation of women from family exploitation, while paying attention to the value of family love
- recognising that women's exploitation results from capitalism, not patriarchy, so it can only be addressed by socialist revolution

He recommended a future society where:

- all domestic labour and care of children, the elderly and sick should be carried out by neighbourhood services run by both sexes
- women would leave domestic isolation to join a workforce reorganised along communist lines, with a shorter working week to encourage mixing within the community
- the disappearance of class divisions would integrate citizens, and both sexes would develop personally through increased social activity as well as through enhanced family life and individual self-realisation

Task 3.3

Consider Zaretsky's plan for the future, particularly the first point. Would everyone welcome such arrangements?

What are the views of Marxist feminists?

Some feminists have agreed with Zaretsky that women face double exploitation, by capitalism *and* patriarchy. Husbands are dominated by their bosses, and much of this burden is transferred onto wives.

Margaret Benston (1972) argued that a woman's domestic labour not only benefits the husband but also indirectly helps his employer. The man who is well fed, well clothed and soothed by his wife is an efficient worker, and the 'warm bath' of family life distracts him from exploitation at work. By virtue of this, the capitalist can make greater profits from the husband's labour, yet the housewife is paid nothing. Benston shared Juliet Mitchell's observation that the family also benefits capitalism by producing future workers, spending years teaching children skills and self-discipline. Learning to accept their father's authority prepares children for obeying their own boss later in life.

Women's domestic responsibilities often leave them available only for part-time work, reducing their bargaining power as employees; consequently, they accept poorly paid, insecure work. Many women, together with ethnic minorities, belong to the **reserve army of labour** — workers willing to fill jobs when they arise but dismissed without much compensation during slumps. Women are generally cheaper to employ and easier to exploit than male workers, who expect better conditions and are likely to join trade unions.

Another link between gender and class conflict is that antagonism between male and female workers, due to power struggles in the family, may prevent them from uniting to overthrow capitalism. Men are more likely to vent their work frustrations on their own wives and children. Open opposition to the boss could mean dismissal, a risk they are unwilling to take because of their families' financial dependence on them, so they remain exploited.

More recently, Christine Delphy and Diana Leonard (in *Familiar Exploitation*, 1992) were influenced by both Marxist and radical feminist ideas. They described the family as a unit in which the male is usually the breadwinner and his dependent wife works unpaid with no contract. She is automatically assigned unlimited housework and is expected to support her husband's business and his emotional and sexual wellbeing. He is the chief decision-maker, controls family finances, takes the best car, the most food, and has to be humoured. Delphy and Leonard claimed this is largely true even when wives work outside the home. Their sample was largely working class, and it may be that middle-class women nowadays might not be so easily browbeaten by their husbands.

Task 3.4

Critics have pointed out that some Marxist feminist arguments seem outdated, as they assume a male breadwinner and a wife at home or working part-time for a secondary wage. Girls are now out-performing boys in some fields and frequently find well-paid employment more easily.

Analyse the other points made above to decide which are still likely to be relevant in modern society.

Socialist feminists Michele Barrett and Mary McIntosh warned against gener-alising about gender roles in view of **family diversity** (variety), but still agreed that families preserve capitalism. In *The Anti-Social Family* (1982), they suggested that government and media promotion of conventional families, known as familism, makes single people feel unsuccessful and isolated, even though the image of cosy family life may be false. Traditional working-class solidarity, such as trade union and socialist party activity, has broken down as people spend more time at home in the privatised family.

> We are not arguing against personal life, or against privacy, but for a better balance between private and public and a private life that is not so demanding and draining and not so all-important. For many people, work is so unrewarding that they centre their lives round their home…Public spaces become shopping precincts where people go only to stock up on the goodies they consume in private…To some extent the solution must involve changing the nature of work and revitalising public life…The closer the emotional ties between the members of the community, the less the need to seek refuge from loneliness in marriage.
>
> M. Barrett and M. McIntosh, *The Anti-Social Family* (1982)

Though some Marxist feminists share the confidence of the writers of the American Socialist Workers' Party resolution that feminists and left-wingers can work together for the benefit of all, Heidi Hartmann (1981) regarded the bond as an uneasy marriage, in which Marxism plays the dominant husband role. Marxism explains capitalist oppression but fails to examine why it is predominantly women who carry the burden of domestic labour and do the most poorly paid jobs. If society were completely reorganised on communist lines, there could still be winners and losers, and it is unlikely that men would be willing to give up their current dominance.

Task 3.5

To what extent did the experience of women under Soviet Communism support Heidi Hartmann's argument?

Summary

- The main focus of Marxists is on class inequality, but they view the family as an important site of exploitation and perpetuation of capitalist values.
- Engels believed that marriage originated at the same time as capitalism.
- Soviet Communists initially tried to dismantle the privatised family to encourage more communal living, causing a variety of problems, especially for women and children.
- Zaretsky recommended that under communism, the domestic chores women

currently undertake should be carried out communally, freeing both sexes to work and enjoy family life on an equal footing.

- Marxist feminists have focused more than traditional Marxists on women's exploitation within the family, identifying the need to challenge patriarchy as well as capitalism.

Task 3.6

Suggest three ways in which, according to Marxists, the traditional family perpetuates capitalism. (6 marks)

Guidance

- This AQA style question requires careful planning. Candidates often lose marks by repeating virtually the same point in different words.
- Decide on three completely different and distinct points before starting to write. Set out each point on a new line to help the marker.
- As 2 marks are available for each point, it is useful to begin with a key term and then amplify it with a brief explanation.
- Do not be tempted to write more than a couple of sentences per point. Save time for the questions carrying higher marks.

Useful websites

- Wikipedia on Marxism
  http://en.wikipedia.org/wiki/Marxism#Marxist_Feminism
- *Gender and History*, Linda Nicholson (1986): helpful chapter on types of Marxist feminism and the women's movement
  www.marxists.org/reference/subject/philosophy/works/us/nichols2.htm

Further reading

- Barrett, M. and McIntosh, M. (1982) *The Anti-Social Family*, Verso.
- Bell, N. and Vogel, E. (eds) (1968) *A Modern Introduction to the Family*, Free Press.

In what ways have industrialisation and globalisation influenced household structures?

This chapter examines changes to the structure of households resulting from economic and cultural changes. The extracts contained in Boxes 4.1 and 4.2 reveal how African families have been tragically disrupted as a result of a particular set of conditions in the postmodern world — global inequalities and ease of travel. According to some sociologists, UK families centuries earlier were fragmented as a result of industrialisation and urbanisation.

Box 4.1

Victoria Climbié leaves her family

Victoria Climbié was born in the Ivory Coast in 1991. She was the fifth of seven children and had a healthy and happy early childhood. She started school at the age of 6 and showed herself to be intelligent and articulate. Perhaps this was why Victoria came to the attention of her father's aunt. Marie-Therese Kouao had lived in France for some years but was visiting the Ivory Coast in 1998. She told Mr and Mrs Climbié that she wished to take a child back to France with her and arrange for his or her education. Victoria was happy to be chosen. Entrusting children to relatives living in Europe who can offer financial and educational opportunities unavailable in the Ivory Coast is not uncommon in Victoria's parents' society. Despite her parents' best intentions, Victoria was soon to die, a victim of horrendous abuse.

Adapted from Victoria Climbié Inquiry
www.victoria-climbie-inquiry.org.uk/finreport/vicstory.htm

Box 4.2

The welfare of African children in the UK

In light of the tragic death of Victoria Climbié, the welfare of migrant African children living in the UK has generated considerable interest within the national press. A BBC investigation that was published in a report by ECPAT UK (End Child Prostitution, Pornography and Trafficking) found that an estimated 10,000 children from west Africa were living with strangers in the UK. Hundreds of west African children had not only been brought illegally to the UK as part of scams for state

Victoria Climbié

benefit, but were also being severely abused. One organisation set up to raise awareness about the welfare of African children both in the UK and their countries of origin is Africans Unite Against Child Abuse (AFRUCA).

Adapted from a report by Sandra Brobbey for Precious online
www.preciousonline.co.uk/reportage/feb02/African.html

Many sociologists view developments in the UK and western European societies in terms of three eras, distinguished by major differences in the institutions and predominant culture, though the cut-off dates and terminology are subject to debate (Box 4.3).

Box 4.3

Eras in UK cultural history

Pre-modernity

- From the beginning of recorded history until about the eighteenth century.
- Most people lived in the countryside, travelled little and accepted traditional hierarchies and religious beliefs.

Modernity

- From the eighteenth century until about the 1950s.
- A period of intellectual enlightenment and rapid social change, with most of the population moving to the towns in response to industrialisation.
- Old hierarchies and beliefs were questioned as people undertook new types of work and became more geographically and socially mobile.
- Some sociologists suggest these changes began earlier with the Reformation.

Chapter 4

> Box 4.3 (continued)
>
> **Postmodernity**
>
> - The current era.
> - Advanced technology such as computers, mass media and rapid international travel have resulted in mass migrations, globalisation, availability of huge amounts of information and alternative ideas and beliefs, allowing more choice of lifestyle but creating a degree of moral confusion.

Historians and sociologists have debated the degree to which the family changed from extended to nuclear as a result of the industrialisation that brought an end to the pre-modern era. Of more current interest is the degree to which households have changed since about 1950 and the possible effects on postmodern society. Each debate will be examined in turn.

How were UK families changed by industrialisation?

Most sociologists agree that industrialisation caused many changes in UK family structure and functions. Before the mid-eighteenth century, most goods were made manually or by simple domestic machines, or produced on a small farm, run (after the feudal system declined) by a classic extended family. This might consist of three generations, for example grandparents, their sons (some married with children) and their unmarried daughters.

According to C. Arensberg and S. Kimball (1940), families were economic units where women performed production tasks that were different from men's but equally essential. Housework and childcare was mainly devolved to older children and the elderly, though they might have productive roles too. The financially dependent housewife had not yet emerged.

Talcott Parsons (1959) argued that the nuclear family, consisting only of parents and their children, emerged as a result of the Industrial Revolution. This was the change from home to factory production because of mechanisation. Farms became bigger and more competitive, and many people moved to towns to work for wages in the growing industries. It suited the needs of manufacturers for families to become smaller units, so this is known as the 'theory of fit'.

Parsons suggested that families changed from extended to nuclear after industrialisation for several reasons:

- It was easier for smaller units to move to where the jobs were, unhampered by responsibilities for other relatives.
- The young sought new types of work, so the vocational training and job opportunities relatives could offer were less useful.
- Eventually, larger organisations (such as schools, hospitals and the welfare state) provided some of the support previously undertaken by kin, leaving fewer functions for the family to perform alone.

William Goode (1963) agreed that industrialisation made living in an extended family less practical. Relatives with varying occupations might adopt different lifestyles, and there could be conflicts of authority if an adult son lived with a father of lower occupational status. People welcomed freedom from obligations to lots of kin, only retaining beneficial contacts. The upper class, for example, might still be able to obtain work for relatives through the 'old boys' network'.

How reliable are historical generalisations?

The assumptions made by Parsons and Goode that families were extended before the industrial revolution and nuclear afterwards have been undermined by close scrutiny of secondary data.

Historian Peter Laslett's 1972 study of family size between 1564 and 1821 showed that, according to parish documents and national statistics, only about 10% of households contained extended kin, similar to the situation in the modern UK. Couples had children relatively late and lives were shorter, so for three generations to live together was rare.

Michael Anderson studied the 1851 census for Preston, Lancashire, a centre for the cotton industry. He found the tendency to live with extended kin was high, because the cost of accommodation could be shared and grandparents cared for children while the parents worked.

Taken together, these studies provide evidence for the predominance of nuclear families before industrialisation and sound reasons for living in extended families in industrialised towns. Therefore, it is dangerous to generalise about historical changes in the family.

Young and Willmott's four-stage family

Historical changes in household structure and size also transformed the roles of family members. In *The Symmetrical Family* (1973), Michael Young and Peter Willmott identified four stages of such changes, while emphasising the coexistence of different forms resulting from local conditions and class differences. Lifestyle changes usually begin in higher social classes and permeate down the social scale in a process of stratified diffusion.

Stage 1: The pre-industrial family

The family was usually a unit of production, with men, women and children working together. The wife typically supervised the dairy, the husband worked more outdoors, and young children commonly helped the same-sex parent, learning skills from them rather than from school. The husband was undisputed master and the marriage was an economic settlement not necessarily built on love. Other relatives and servants might live in the household, helping in the family economy and with infant care.

The family as a unit of production is now rare in the modern UK, except in farming communities.

Stage 2: The early industrial family

In the early factories, women and children worked alongside men. However, this practice ended after the introduction of Victorian laws forbidding child labour and restricting women's hours and pay. The result was the gendered division of labour: men in paid work and women as housewives. This was common until the mid-twentieth century and was examined in detail in Young and Willmott's *Family and Kinship in East London* (1961).

Though families were frequently nuclear, relatives often lived in the same streets in industrialised areas, maintaining kinship networks, especially among women. Confined to the home, young mothers sought support from their own mothers, depending upon the Demeter (mother and daughter) bond. Mothers and daughters would visit each other on a daily basis.

As a result, bonds between spouses weakened and men tended to spend their leisure time in working-men's clubs and public houses instead of with their families. Nineteenth-century accounts suggest men were more inclined to beat women and children now they were no longer wage earners, as there was less need to humour them.

D. H. Lawrence's autobiographical novel *Sons and Lovers* (1913) reflects this pattern of family relationships. The father, a coalminer, feels excluded from the close bond between his wife and young sons and spends his evenings with workmates in the public house. He comes home late to an angry wife, having spent most of his wages. The poor welcome goads him to physical violence, increasing the rift between him, the sole breadwinner, and the rest of the family who are his dependents.

From 1880, schooling became compulsory, yet fees were charged until 1891, creating for working-class families the double burden of paying for education while missing out on the earnings from children's casual work. Having ten or more children was common, so many families lived in poverty until the children became self-sufficient. As they were sent off every weekday to a special institution exclusively for their peer group, they could no longer be regarded as mini adults.

Stage 3: The privatised family

During the twentieth century, manufacturing diminished and employment in the professions and service industries increased. Younger generations moved away from the centres of dock labouring, mining and ship building, where their parents and grandparents were once employed, to seek different types of work, and this geographical and social mobility weakened kinship ties.

From the mid-twentieth century, welfare benefits and better wages meant nuclear families were financially less dependent on other relatives. As they could afford to make their homes more pleasant, often by DIY improvements, working-class men were keener to spend leisure time at home and family bonds grew stronger. Improved transport, eventually including car ownership, enabled prosperous couples to seek housing in pleasant suburbs further from their natal families. The nuclear family had become a site of consumption instead of one of production.

Improvements in contraception (especially after the NHS made the pill available in 1961) and wider acceptance of birth control, reduced the years women spent in child bearing from about 15 years to an average of 4. This, along with improved education and the influence of feminism, encouraged more women to undertake paid work, expecting their husbands to help with housework and childcare. Young and Willmott described the resulting arrangement as the **symmetrical family**, as both partners shared responsibility for earning money, household chores and childcare, though they might perform different tasks.

> The couple and their children are very much centred on the home, especially when the children are young. They can...share so much together, because they spend so much of their time together in the same space. Life has...become more 'privatised'.
>
> M. Young and P. Willmott, *The Symmetrical Family* (1973)

Despite the cosy, apparently egalitarian family conveyed here, studies of conjugal roles have questioned the degree to which men help in the home and involve their wives in decisions.

Stage 4: The managing director family

Young and Willmott identified a fourth stage, which they predicted might become more widespread as international trade expanded. They interviewed managing directors who led work-centred lives and spent long periods of time away from home. Unless their wives also had demanding jobs and could afford au pairs, they were left to cope with the children. This revealed a movement away from the symmetrical family and closer to the stage 2 family in terms of segregated gender roles.

Several of Young and Willmott's predictions have indeed occurred:

- With globalisation, more workers frequently travel abroad and see less of their families.
- Young wives are less prepared to accept the burden of housework while their husbands travel.
- Women have increasingly sought rewarding employment and experience role strain, torn between family responsibilities and career.
- Children see less of their parents who may bring work home or work long hours for higher incomes.
- Wider leisure interests encourage men, women and children to spend more leisure time apart (especially teenagers).
- Divorce has increased, sometimes resulting from disputes as working women expect husbands to help more domestically and couples disagree about where to live so they can both access employment.

Indeed, Young and Willmott suggested that widespread family breakdown could be imminent and discussed whether alternative arrangements, such as the kibbutz, might need to be substituted if the family ceased to be the sort of haven described in Stage 3.

Task 4.1

Draw a chart with four columns to represent the family stages identified by Young and Willmott. Make notes on the main features and incorporate relevant aspects of pre-modernity, modernity and postmodernity identified earlier in the chapter. This is best done on a computer, so that you can add in more details as you read on.

Has industrialisation affected the family globally?

Though the discussion of industrialising the UK appears to be of little contemporary relevance, similar developments are now affecting family life in developing countries:

- In rural areas in African countries such as Tanzania, men leave their wives and children to farm the family plot while they seek more lucrative work in industrial towns or growing cash crops for the international market.
- Sometimes young people of both sexes desert the land, leaving behind the elderly who are unable to farm it effectively.
- Many cities in developing countries have grown rapidly, with the poorest inhabitants living in illegal settlements or overcrowded shanties with no access to water, sewerage and health services. Children living in the shanties are 50 times more likely to die before the age of 5 than those in developed countries.

Task 4.2

Read the extract and consider the questions that follow.

All over the Third World, millions of people who were once peasant farmers are abandoning the countryside, having been driven from the land by rich commercial farmers, drought, wide-scale flooding for hydroelectric schemes, lack of work and population explosions. But when they get to the cities they find that life is often a good deal worse.

João Andre's poor family farmed other people's land in what was once the heartland of Brazil's plantation prosperity, but mechanised farming was being introduced to the area, producing soya beans for export to Europe. Tractors meant fewer jobs for labourers and no land for subsistence farming so he was forced to take a low-paid job in São Paulo and build his family a shack in the *favela* (slum).

…More than 200 families appear in São Paulo daily looking for a job. Most of them have no money, little education and few marketable skills. Those who do find jobs try to find rented rooms in the old tenement houses. The rest try to find an unused corner in one of the teeming *favelas*. Many, especially the children and teenagers, cannot find even that and live on the streets where, with no jobs available, prostitution and crime become norms. For a large number it ends in violent death; there are estimated to be 700,000 street children in Rio de Janeiro alone and every month thirty or forty of them are killed by death squads of policemen or vigilantes cleaning up the streets.

Adapted from Paul Vallely, *Promised Lands: Stories of Power and Poverty in the Third World* (1992)

(1) What effects is the drift to the cities described above likely to be having on:
- the extended family
- the nuclear family
- life expectancy

Task 4.2 (continued)

(2) Find out about the effects of the Enclosure Acts on UK country dwellers from 1750, using websites such as **www.countrylovers.co.uk/places/histlan4.htm**. Compare the enclosure movement with the situation in contemporary Brazil.

(3) Was there an equivalent of the Brazilian street children in the London slums during the nineteenth century? Charles Dickens's *Oliver Twist* (or the film *Oliver!*) should provide a clue..

In Brazil, mechanised farming has meant fewer jobs for labourers and no subsistence farming; many are forced to accept low-paid jobs in the cities and to live in shacks in the *favelas* (slums)

In many developing countries, young women are tempted away from their natal families to work for transnational companies in export processing zones. Female workers, who are often housed in single-sex barracks near the factory so that they can work longer hours, are preferred to males because they are generally more nimble fingered and less assertive about demanding a living wage. Often the working conditions lead to deteriorating eyesight and failing health, so the employees are sacked and, having no savings from their low wages and no union rights, they may fall into prostitution.

How has globalisation affected the family?

Easier international travel, combined with global inequalities, has resulted in major economic immigration of the young from developing to developed countries, with males often establishing themselves for several years before sending for family members. South Asians settling in the UK from the 1950s were involved in this chain migration, eventually bringing over wives and children but frequently leaving extended kin behind in the country of origin. Roger Ballard (1990) found that small UK houses were unsuited to the multigenerational households typical of the Punjab, Gujarat and Bengal, though sometimes extended kin managed to buy adjoining houses or live close by. Where relatives remained behind in south Asia, families maintained frequent contact, travelling to and from the subcontinent and sometimes sending back money to the elderly.

Some countries such as Cambodia are so desperately poor that parents sell their babies to orphanages for as little as £15, to be adopted later as orphans by couples from developed countries such as the UK.

Parents in many developing countries send children to industrialised nations to improve their education, as in the tragic case of Toni-Ann Byfield who, like Victoria Climbié, came to the UK for a better life. Born in a poor area of Jamaica, she was sent by her mother to stay with relatives in Birmingham. While social services tried to resolve where she should live, she was murdered in the home of a drug dealer.

Young women from developing countries may be tricked by promises of lucrative, legitimate work in Europe but find themselves sold into prostitution,

Box 4.4

Madonna 'adopts child in Africa'

Pop star Madonna has adopted a 1-year-old boy in Malawi. The boy's father, Yohane Banda, said: 'I am the father of David, who has been adopted. I am very very happy because as you can see there is poverty in this village and I know he will be very well looked after in America.' He told reporters that his wife died a month after the baby's birth from childbirth complications. Since then the child had been cared for at the Home of Hope Orphan Care Centre in Mchinji.

Rex Features

Adapted from BBC news online (11 October 2006) http://news.bbc.co.uk/1/hi/entertainment/6039380.stm

and some destitute families knowingly enslave their children for this purpose. However, the greatest disruption to the family in parts of the developing world may not be globalisation but AIDS.

In *Full Circles: Geographies on Women over the Life Course* (1993), Cindi Katz and Janice Monk discussed how global capitalism has led to displacements of population from rural areas in the Caribbean and South America to the industrialised economies of North America.

Canada has an immigration policy encouraging lone women workers, so Caribbean women may leave their children with relatives and neighbours back home while working as domestics for Canadian working mothers. This is made possible by the west Indian 'houseyard system', a traditional communal living arrangement involving a cluster of simple houses and outbuildings around a central activity area. The houseyard, inhabited by as many as 30 relatives and friends, is often headed by an older woman with some of her adult children (most often female) and their children, sometimes the daughters' current partners, and cousins with their children. As girls get older, they are supervised to prevent relationships with men with poor prospects, but these bonds are viewed as temporary.

> There is little expectation, on the part of the girl, her family or the mate, that the relationship will be life long. The girl will, in most cases, continue to live in her customary yard, with the male only visiting several times a week and taking some of his meals there. Girls may have their first babies as early as age fourteen and fifteen; but often their mothering role is rather limited after the first few weeks because childcare is willingly taken over by older kin or unrelated yard residents, especially females, but also males. Whereas in the past young mothers might have worked as agricultural wage labourers, now they tend to return to school or jobs in the service or industrial sectors of the economy. In fact the houseyard system, which provides shelter and opportunities to cooperate in childcare, gardening, animal tending, laundry and food preparation, allows young women to be astonishingly independent, despite the early onset of motherhood.
>
> C. Katz and J. Monk, *Full Circles: Geographies on Women over the Life Course* (1993)

This independence extends to allowing mothers to migrate abroad for several years, sending back money to their children and elderly relatives left behind in the houseyard.

Task 4.3

Compare the effects of industrialisation and globalisation on the extended family of the Caribbean houseyard with the effects of industrialisation on western families identified by Parsons and Goode.

Has the extended family disappeared from postmodern Britain?

Although most Britons do not live in extended families, adults usually keep in regular contact with their parents. Support and practical help are exchanged, especially between mothers and daughters; this is continued evidence of the Demeter bond. Janet Finch, in *Family Obligations and Social Change* (1989), identified five types of assistance:

- **Economic support**: parents frequently help adult children with loans, gifts, finding employment for them and through their wills.
- **Accommodation**: many young adults still live with parents or return temporarily after domestic crises. Only 6% of the elderly live with their children, though the percentage is higher among some ethnic minorities.
- **Personal care**: elderly and disabled parents are frequently cared for by daughters, and younger disabled adults by parents.
- **Practical support**: grandmothers often help daughters with childcare and domestic tasks. About a quarter of pre-school children are cared for by grandparents while mothers work — far more than go to nurseries or to registered child minders.
- **Emotional support**: young mothers often seek their own mothers' advice on childcare and important purchases. As they mature, people are more likely to seek emotional support from friends instead.

Finch therefore discovered that there were many ways in which grandparents continued to assist children and grandchildren, and help sometimes flowed back the other way. Most of those interviewed felt older generations should aid younger family members, but far fewer thought the young were obliged to help their elderly family members.

Other studies reveal that, regardless of social class and area, adults keep in frequent contact with parents and siblings, and often give practical help. Fathers and fathers-in-law often help with the expenses of new babies or housing.

How should the nuclear family's bonds with kin best be described?

Clearly, Parsons's description of isolated nuclear families has to be interpreted with caution. He meant that nuclear families are economically independent of wider kin on a day-to-day basis, unlike the multigenerational farm. However, as 'isolated' might be taken to imply no contact with other kin, Eugene Litwak (1975) proposed the term modified extended family, instead. This differs from the classic extended family living together, but involves regular support and contact by telephone, post and visits (and nowadays by e-mail and text messaging on mobile phones).

Graham Allan (1985) also distinguished modern families from classic extended ones because their sense of obligation in crises extends only to inner or 'elementary' members, not to uncles, cousins and more distant kin. He preferred the term modified elementary family, as it indicates the limitations within which members feel the need to offer help and keep in close touch.

Comparing kinship ties with the past

Janet Finch cautioned against contrasting the modern families' restricted sense of obligation to wider kin with the situation in a former 'golden age'. Though there is evidence of relatives housing orphans and elderly people not in their elementary family, they were often expected to work in return and to share costs. These arrangements were for mutual advantage in conditions different from today's. Jane Austen's novel *Mansfield Park* and Charlotte Brontë's *Jane Eyre* provide examples of poor or orphaned girls sent to live with prosperous relatives, but in each case they were treated as inferiors.

Studies of historical changes in the family (such as Willmott and Young's) need interpreting cautiously. The closeness to kin associated with their Stage-2 family has not vanished entirely. Willmott himself found in north London in 1986 that two thirds of married couples with children saw relatives at least weekly, as well as receiving frequent help from them.

In 1996, Margaret O'Brien and Deborah Jones returned to the east London of Willmott and Young's 1950s study and discovered that 47% of children had maternal grandparents living locally and 20% had over ten local relatives. Despite a greater variety of lifestyles than in the 1950s, including more dual-earner and lone-parent families, the amount of contact with kin had changed little.

Novels such as Dickens's *A Christmas Carol* (1843) present an ideal picture of the big, happy, united family, but it is important to remember that since that time women are far less likely to die in childbirth, life expectancy and standards of health have increased, poor children no longer have to work and couples have more choice about how many children to have and whether to stay together. Family diversity as a result of such choice will be the subject of the next chapter.

Summary

- Industrialisation has affected family structures in Europe and, more recently, in the developing world.

- Parsons and Goode suggested that when UK families moved from rural to urban employment, they often left elderly and other kin behind, resulting in a change from extended to nuclear arrangements.
- However, Laslett found evidence of predominantly nuclear families well before industrialisation, and Anderson found extended families in industrial Lancashire.
- In the developing world, many rural areas have been taken over by mechanised farming for cash crops, driving peasants off the land in a similar way to the UK enclosure movements. Families are split as people gravitate to mega cities.
- Globalisation and global inequalities give rise to horrendous situations such as the selling of babies and sex slavery.
- Some household arrangements, such as the Caribbean houseyard, are flexible enough to allow family members to work in more industrialised countries while others care for their children.
- The modified extended family refers to families staying in frequent touch with extended kin. Young and Willmott and Finch found evidence of such patterns of mutual obligation in the twentieth century.

Task 4.4

Assess the view that, despite industrialisation and urbanisation, the extended family never disappeared and continues to thrive today. (20 marks)

Guidance

- The key word 'assess' makes it clear that this is a debate with at least two sides. It is important to organise your ideas effectively and to evaluate the different sides of the argument (AO2 evaluation skills). It could be useful to divide your essay into two sections, discussing the effects of industrialisation and urbanisation on UK families in the past and on families in developing countries in more recent times (AO1 knowledge and understanding).
- Begin by defining the extended family, comparing the classic extended family living under the same roof with the modified extended family identified by Litwak. The ambiguity of the term lies at the heart of the debate (AO2 skills of analysis and intepretation).
- The most controversial debate is between supporters of Parsons and Goode, who suggest that UK families ceased to be extended after the Industrial Revolution, and Anderson, Young and Willmott and Finch, who described close family networks and obligations between adults of different generations long after that period.

Task 4.4 (continued)

- Examiners welcome examples from other cultures (AO1). Young people moving
  from rural areas to industrialised areas leaving the elderly behind threatens the
  extended family, yet the case study of the Caribbean houseyard demonstrates
  that mothers can only work abroad because the extended family can be relied
  upon to look after their children.
- Remember to include a thoughtful conclusion, perhaps reiterating that the debate
  hinges on the interpretation of the phrase 'extended family' (AO2).

Research suggestion

You could replicate the research of Margaret O'Brien and Deborah Jones by
asking young people how many relatives they have living locally and to what
extent they form a supportive network. You will need to decide what counts as
local, and may wish to see whether social class, ethnicity and other factors make
a difference.

Useful websites

- 'Sociology Stuff'— select family section then click on 'Family and History'
  www.homestead.com/rouncefield/frontpage.html
- Wikipedia on the Industrial Revolution, especially the sections on social
  effects, some of which were very positive
  http://en.wikipedia.org/wiki/Industrial_Revolution
- Human Rights Watch: street children
  http://hrw.org/children/street.htm
- National Geographic Magazine site on mega cities with connected links
  http://magma.nationalgeographic.com/ngm/0211/feature3/?fs=www3.nationalgeographic
  .com&fs=plasma.nationalgeographic.com

Further reading

- Finch, J. (1989) *Family Obligations and Social Change*, Polity Press.
- Katz, C. and Monk, J. (eds) (1993) *Full Circles: Geographies on Women over the Life Course*, Routledge.
- Vallely, P. (1992) *Promised Lands: Stories of Power and Poverty in the Third World*, Fount Paperbacks and Christian Aid.
- Young, M. and Willmott, P. (1973) *The Symmetrical Family*, Routledge and Kegan Paul.

Chapter 5

How have patterns of family life changed in recent times?

This chapter examines in detail recent changes in religious and moral attitudes that have given rise to greater social acceptance of divorce, remarriage, cohabitation and births outside marriage, together with changes in family size. The task below will alert you to these changes. Other aspects of diversity, such as the growth of homosexual and single-person households and the different family structures of ethnic minorities, are discussed in Chapter 6, where the effects of government policies on diversity are also considered.

Task 5.1

Consider how the following aspects of postmodern (or late-modern) culture are likely to produce family diversity in the contemporary UK:

- **Secularisation**: the weakening of traditional religious beliefs and practices, mainly concerning sexual morality, especially in communities that were previously Christian.
- **Relativism**: the view that different types of people are entitled to lead different lifestyles, instead of following a prescribed pattern upheld as absolutely right.
- **Individualism**: people are encouraged to seek personal happiness; obligations to please wider kin are less pressing than in the past.
- **Globalisation**: increased immigration from beyond Europe since the Second World War, bringing distinctive family patterns and moral attitudes.
- **Liberation movements**: women, homosexuals, youth and the elderly have campaigned for enhanced rights and dignity.
- **Demographic changes**: people live longer, generally healthier lives; many women choose to postpone childbirth until their career is established and also tend to have smaller families; as a result they are sometimes more economically independent.
- **Extended education**: experienced by more young people, prolonging their financial dependence on parents.

The 'cereal packet family'

Some years ago, UK advertisers marketed 'family packs' of their products, using promotional photographs of a nuclear family consisting of white parents living with their own children, usually one boy and one girl. This became known as the cereal packet family, 'Oxo family' or conventional family. Corresponding television commercials usually implied the husband was the breadwinner while the wife stayed at home.

A typical 'cereal packet family' consists of white parents living with their own children, usually one boy and one girl

In reality, five common patterns of parenting exist today, consisting of children living with:

- married parents
- an unmarried couple
- one divorced or separated parent
- a married parent with a new partner
- a never-married parent

A further arrangement likely to become increasingly wide-spread is children being cared for by homosexual adults, especially those in a civil partnership.

In 1992, Robert and Rhona Rapoport observed that the proportion of house-holds consisting of married couples with dependent children had declined to below a quarter, compared with 38% in 1961. They viewed this change as evidence not of family failure but of availability of choice. Greater employment opportunities for women and more liberal ideas about family diversity mean that people can opt for arrangements that suit them. Allowing unhappy couples to divorce, financially assisting lone parents and not stigmatising the illegitimate are signs of a humane society.

While feminists and liberals tend to agree, New Right thinkers and followers of traditional religious beliefs are concerned about the decline of the conventional family. To what extent has this stereotypical family disappeared from the contemporary UK? What have been the effects of these changes on family members and society as a whole?

Individualism and the importance of love

Graham Allan and Graham Crow (2001) explored the connections between family diversity and the individualism mentioned in Task 5.1. They compared pre-industrial society, when parents and other kin had considerable influence over the behaviour of young adults, with the later period of individualised wage labour:

> Because the younger generation relied less for their means of livelihood on resources which parents controlled, they could more readily disregard the latter's wishes…the nuclear family became increasingly independent of wider kin. This in turn encouraged the development of personal attraction, and hence romantic love, as the major rationale for marital selection…Other factors were undoubtedly important — the need for economic security, the desire for sexual expression, or whatever — but the way marriage was explained was by references to the feelings which existed between the couple.
>
> G. Allan and G. Crow, *Families, Households and Society* (2001)

Gradually, love became the supreme focus of self-realisation, whether through marriage or other relationships:

> Those who do not experience such love, or whose love has not been fully realised, often have a sense of loss or of incompleteness, of an emotional void which can only partly be compensated for by other forms of relationship. As Giddens (1991) has argued, in late modernity the notion of expressing the self through exclusive, intimate relationships has attained far greater cultural prominence than it had even a generation ago.
>
> G. Allan and G. Crow, *Families, Households and Society* (2001)

Thus, romantic love has become for many a life goal, but an inherently unstable one. Falling in love motivates alternative arrangements such as cohabitation, while falling out of it is offered as sufficient justification to terminate partnerships. Anthony Giddens (1991) has described the current era as characterised by people reflecting on what they think will make them happy and prioritising it, as opposed to following the will of God or social conventions. As people seek to develop 'the self as a project', this inevitably leads to diversity of lifestyle choices.

These observations reveal the limitations of functionalist and Marxist perspectives, which describe only the impact of major social structures on family arrangements. Certainly these are important, as family lifestyles still differ between different social classes and between ethnic and religious groups. However, equally important nowadays is the notion of **agency** — the individual's ability to make choices in his or her personal life. Another factor is generation, as people who grow up in particular decades usually absorb the attitudes towards personal conduct prevalent at that time. Giddens coined the term structuration to refer to the combined influence on individual behaviour of social structure and choice of action.

Task 5.2

Examine the figure below, which relates to individuals over the age of 16. In view of earlier comments about family diversity, what do you find surprising about the proportions of people living in different arrangements?

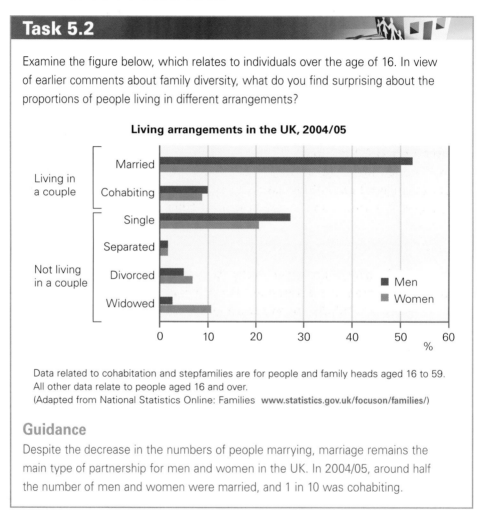

Living arrangements in the UK, 2004/05

Data related to cohabitation and stepfamilies are for people and family heads aged 16 to 59. All other data relate to people aged 16 and over.
(Adapted from National Statistics Online: Families **www.statistics.gov.uk/focuson/families/**)

Guidance

Despite the decrease in the numbers of people marrying, marriage remains the main type of partnership for men and women in the UK. In 2004/05, around half the number of men and women were married, and 1 in 10 was cohabiting.

Why can family statistics be misleading?

The figure accompanying Task 5.2 gives a more conventional impression of family structures than the statistics provided by Robert and Rhona Rapoport. This shows that it is important to distinguish between statistics for individuals, partnerships, families and households. The reasons become clear if you imagine focusing on a conventional household consisting of a married couple with three children and another household solely occupied by a divorcee. Of this sample you could say five out of six *people* live as part of a conventional family or only half the *households* are occupied by conventional families. Scaled up as part of a national survey, this could be confusing. Sociologists or policy makers might choose either method of measuring social behaviour, depending on whether they wanted to present a picture of family stability or decline.

Has marriage become less popular?

Although married couples constituted the main family type in 2004/05, the number of married-couple families fell by 4% (0.5 million) between 1996 and 2004. In this same period the number of cohabiting-couple families increased by over 50% to 2.2 million.

Even though marriage is still popular, the average age at which people first marry in England and Wales has risen by almost 7 years over the last three decades, to 31 for men and 29 for women in 2004.

Why do people marry later?

Reasons for delaying marriage are likely to include:

- **Longer education**: the government target is for 50% of young people to go to university by 2010. Few people consider marriage while they are dependent on student loans and parental support.
- **Feminism and equal opportunities**: women often wish to establish a career before settling down to have a family. Mothers give birth on average 3 years later than in the 1970s.
- **Decline in traditional manual work for males**: young men are less likely to have sufficient income to establish a family than in the prosperous post-war period.
- **Higher material expectations**: many young people delay marriage until they can afford mortgage payments on their own house. Often they wait until they have saved enough to maintain a good standard of living, even if the wife stops work to have children.
- **Changing moral attitudes and effective birth control**: in the past, illegitimacy was stigmatised, so couples who wished to be sexually active married young. Now the risks of unwanted pregnancy are reduced, the stigma is less and cohabitation (living together unmarried) is regarded by many as an acceptable compromise. As with marriage, women tend to cohabit at younger ages than men. Women aged between 16 and 24 were over twice as likely as men to cohabit in 2004/05.

- **Secularisation**: a survey in 2001 found that people in the UK who defined themselves as having no religion were the most likely to be cohabiting (16% of 16- to 24-year-olds), whereas Sikhs, Hindus and Muslims were the least likely to do so.

Why has cohabitation increased?

Allan and Crow (2001) noted the difficulties of identifying cohabitation for research purposes as it can be a gradual process, with a couple increasingly spending more time together while sometimes maintaining two properties. Cohabitation may be an important commitment and involve taking on a joint mortgage. It may be undertaken as a trial marriage or it can be merely a brief arrangement that ends when, for example, the couple leave university or one finds work elsewhere or decides to travel. As cohabitation is not officially registered or terminated, statistics are unreliable.

Nevertheless, evidence suggests that it has become increasingly popular in the past 50 years. Though the 1960s were commonly regarded as a period of sexual liberation, General Household Survey figures indicate that of those who married for the first time in the late 1960s, only 5% admitted to living together first. Sexual relationships between seriously committed unmarried couples were probably widespread but were carried on clandestinely. In contrast, the General Household Survey of 1997 found that almost 30% of non-married women aged between 20 and 39 were cohabiting.

Allan and Crow suggested several reasons for the increased popularity of cohabitation, some of which overlap with reasons for delaying marriage:

- There has been a change in attitude to sexual expression since the 1960s.

> The dominant message prior to this period was that virginity mattered, especially for women; they should 'save themselves' for the person with whom they wanted to share the rest of their lives…Sexual intercourse…should be resisted for fear of losing 'respect' as a consequence. This particular moral perspective received general support from all sources: schools, churches, media, families.
>
> G. Allan and G. Crow, *Families, Households and Society* (2001)

- The NHS (Family Planning) Act was passed in 1967, making effective contraception readily accessible to unmarried women, and the abortion laws were liberalised in the same year.
- When young people who grew up in the 1960s became parents themselves, they were less anxious to limit their children's sexual experience than previous generations had been.

- More young people now leave home for reasons other than marriage. As many go to university or rent rooms in shared houses, it is easier for couples to cohabit.
- With the increase in marriage break-ups, more separated couples cohabit with new partners while awaiting divorce or through reluctance to commit themselves to another official union. Thus, the symbolism of marriage as a union for life no longer holds the same power, and few people regard cohabitation as 'living in sin'. Behaviour regarded as acceptable for the previously married gradually began to be adopted by single couples.
- Nowadays, building societies and private landlords show little interest in the marital status of house buyers and tenants, whereas in the past they often refused to deal with those not considered 'respectable'.

Allan and Crow stressed that tolerant attitudes towards cohabitation are less typical of some religious minorities in the UK. They also noted some ways in which cohabiting couples exhibit different attitudes and patterns of behaviour from married couples:

- The cohabiting couple have not yet made an irretrievable decision, so they generally maintain more independence. They are more conscious of individual rights and not taking each other for granted. Nevertheless, for many the emphasis may be more on commitment and time spent together than on independence; in 1996, 60% of cohabitations were estimated to result in marriage, though the proportion shows signs of decline.
- Cohabiting partners emphasise that the nature of their relationship is of their own construction and they are less inclined than married couples to follow traditional patterns in the domestic division of labour. However, if they have children, the need to divide roles more conventionally is often felt.

Why has the divorce rate increased?

The divorce rate in the UK has increased dramatically since the 1969 Divorce Reform Act made it possible to dissolve a marriage on grounds of irretrievable breakdown. Chapter 6 provides details of earlier divorce legislation for comparison purposes and discusses whether the government's decision to make divorce easier simply reflected the fact that many marriages were already failing or whether it encouraged more people to divorce who would otherwise have made the best of their marriages.

Historians suggest the changes can be traced further back to the Enlightenment, when the rights of individuals began to be asserted above the authority and welfare of the communities to which they belonged. Marriage gradually became less of an economic arrangement between families and more of a personal relationship between two people, based on romantic love. Inevitably, this is an ideal that is unlikely to be long lasting for most couples, as Ronald Fletcher observed:

> Even if full 'compatibility' is not successfully achieved by the partners in a marriage (and, whatever it is, can it ever be?), and even if 'love' becomes somewhat dimmed amongst the vacuum cleaners and the electric washing machines, this in itself cannot be held to cancel out the duties which parents have towards their children, nor does it obliterate the love and concern they have for them. Finally it does not constitute a supreme ground for dissolving a marriage. Parenthood involves duties to children which must be taken into account whatever the personal relationship of wife and husband.
>
> R.Fletcher, *The Family and Marriage in Britain* (1966)

Many people nowadays would disagree with Fletcher, arguing their own right to personal happiness and questioning whether, if the parents are unhappy, their children will thrive. Some argue that a peaceful upbringing with one parent is preferable to growing up in a quarrelling conventional family.

The decision to divorce relates also to social climate. As with homosexual part-nerships, cohabitation and births outside marriage, as more people are open about these activities, they begin to seem less deviant to others. New norms of behaviour develop and are less stigmatised, except among those groups in the population retaining traditional attitudes. For the majority, the secular indi-vidualism and tolerance of difference of postmodern culture mean that, in personal relationships, almost 'anything goes'.

Current patterns of divorce

By 2004, there were 1.6 million divorced men and 2.2 million divorced women in the UK, compared with 187,000 divorced men and 296,000 women in 1971. One in 5 people divorcing in 2005 had a previous marriage that ended in divorce.

However, the divorce rate has levelled off in recent years and even fell in 2005, especially among the under-40s, perhaps because more people marry later or cohabit instead. This makes predictions difficult, but it seems likely that about 40% of couples currently marrying will eventually divorce. Cohabiting rela-tionships dissolve more frequently than marriages and, if long term, may cause almost as much emotional and economic disruption when they fail, especially where children are involved.

In 2005, almost 7 in 10 divorces in England and Wales were granted to the wife. Women were most likely to be granted a divorce on the grounds of unreasonable behaviour (53%), whereas for men, the most likely reason was 2 years' separation with consent (32%). Jessie Bernard (1976) interpreted such figures to suggest that marriage is less satisfying to women than to men, because of the domestic drudgery and loss of status. However, Allan and Crow suggested a more practical reason. As women are more likely to look after children when parents separate, it is more important to them to obtain a satisfactory legal and economic settlement. Men may have less to lose by letting the situation drift.

What factors correlate highly with divorce?

Genuine reasons why couples divorce may not be the same as the grounds stated officially, and the subject is too distressing and subjective to have been the focus of many sociological studies. Nevertheless, predisposing factors can be identified by comparing divorced couples with those who have stayed together. Divorce is more likely to occur in the following circumstances:

- where marriages occur early, particularly among teenagers — the partners lack life experience and material resources, and their marriage has to last longer than when people marry later in life
- where couples differ from each other in social class, education, religion, age or ethnicity
- where the woman participates in the labour market, as this increases her independence, the likelihood of meeting other men and the stress of combining work and family life
- where the husband is unemployed, the couple are materially or socially disadvantaged or one partner is disabled or psychologically unstable
- where there has been a premarital birth or cohabitation prior to marriage, probably because this reflects less traditional attitudes; a previously cohabiting couple may find the conventions and legal commitment of marriage more confining
- where one partner has been married before, perhaps because of lowered expectations or the complications of a previous family

What are the effects of divorce?

How are children affected?

There are approximately as many children experiencing their parents' divorce every year as there are divorces. It was estimated in 1997 that 28% of children had experienced parental divorce by the age of 16. As divorce has become

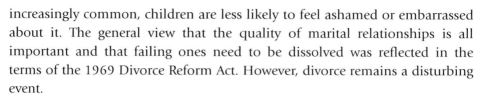

increasingly common, children are less likely to feel ashamed or embarrassed about it. The general view that the quality of marital relationships is all important and that failing ones need to be dissolved was reflected in the terms of the 1969 Divorce Reform Act. However, divorce remains a disturbing event.

> It is a highly emotional and generally painful process, generating feelings of failure, anger, loss, blame, guilt, rejection, loneliness and self doubt…Where there are dependent children, these feelings are compounded by worries over how the separation will affect them. When there has been domestic violence or child abuse, the separation may be seen positively, but for the majority a desire to protect the child's wellbeing, both short-term and long-term, generates additional tensions to an already stressful situation…Issues of financial provision frequently lead to high levels of conflict as standards of living are inevitably compromised when a household divides in two.
>
> G. Allan and G. Crow, *Families, Households and Society* (2001)

How the parents handle their relationships with each other and their children in the lead up to the divorce and its aftermath are more important influences on the emotional wellbeing of the children than the fact of the divorce itself. However, even if the parents protect the child from their decision until it can no longer be hidden, lack of understanding of the causes of the marriage break up often leads children to blame their own behaviour and assume an unnecessary burden of guilt. Anxiety about the future is difficult to assuage when the parents themselves may have little idea of how their lives will be reorganised. For many children, their parents' divorce will involve:

- coping with their own grief and that of their parents and siblings
- reduced income, often leading to poverty; teenagers in particular may find it frustrating being unable to afford fashionable items
- moving house and school and leaving friends behind
- poor quality accommodation; lone parents are far more likely to live in rented accommodation than two-parent families, and this is frequently unsatisfactory for children (such accommodation may be council flats without gardens or temporary bed and breakfast accommodation)
- educational and health problems arising from distraction and stress
- seeing little of, or losing touch with, the non-resident parent and his or her kin
- spending more time unsupervised and having to undertake some adult responsibilities; this might be beneficial, instilling pride in the effective accomplishment of a useful role, although there could also be negative consequences, such as parental neglect, lack of encouragement with school work or a drift into delinquency

How are adults affected?

Women's economic situation worsens dramatically after divorce, while that of men is affected to a much lesser extent. In terms of health, however, divorced men seemingly do less well than divorced women, with men tending to have higher morbidity [illness] and mortality rates.

Kathleen Kiernan and Ganka Mueller in *Changing Britain: Families and Households in the 1990s* (ed. Susan McRae) (1999)

Task 5.3

Why do you think that, when married couples split up, women tend to suffer more financially but men's health declines?

Guidance

Bear in mind that women are far more likely to take primary responsibility for the children.

Having less money than before may discourage divorced women from going out socially, and their changed circumstances tend to distance them from married friends. Eventually, they tend to form new friendships with other separated and divorced people.

The Children Act 1989 encouraged co-parenting after divorce, with both parents involved in many aspects of their child's life. However, such arrangements entail high levels of consultation and cooperation, which are difficult to achieve, especially if the parents wish to make a clean break from each other.

How have patterns of childbearing changed?

Family size

In mid-Victorian times, the average UK family had about six children, whereas now the average is only 1.64. Ronald Fletcher (1966) suggested economic reasons for the change, such as the fact that after the introduction of Victorian laws forbidding child labour, young children were no longer able to work, and instead families had to pay for their education.

In addition, women were becoming more independent and prepared to question tradition. Whereas earlier family size was regarded as the will of God, secular thinkers such as Annie Besant developed a different outlook.

©Mary Evans Picture Library/Alamy

Annie Besant advocated birth control

Despite a court case accusing her of obscenity, she wrote and published *The Laws of Population* in 1877, advocating birth control. The controversial idea became increasingly acceptable among the educated classes and gradually permeated down to the working class.

Ironically, there is now concern that the UK birth rate has declined below replacement level, as in the future a smaller proportion of workers will need to support a larger proportion of elderly people. Factors such as the current high cost of university education may discourage middle-class couples from having more than one or two children. Families are now likened to beanpoles, as later mortality can result in four generations coexisting, while the birth of fewer children makes the family tree look tall and thin.

There is some evidence of unintentional childlessness, as women delay childbirth until their late thirties and then find it difficult to conceive. Environmental pollution may also be affecting fertility, and recent dystopian novels, such as Margaret Atwood's *The Handmaid's Tale* (1985) and P. D. James's *The Children of Men* (1992), paint alarming pictures of societies virtually without children.

On the other hand, reproductive technology is making parenthood possible for couples who in the past would have remained childless. This can sometimes make family life possible in unconventional circumstances. This was illustrated in a recent episode of the radio soap opera *The Archers*, where a female friend of Ian, a homosexual, offered to have his baby by artificial insemination so that Ian and his male partner could bring up a child.

Births outside marriage

The proportion of UK households headed by a lone parent with dependent children has more than doubled since the early 1970s. Until the mid-1980s, a large part of the rise was due to divorce. More recently, the increased proportion of births outside marriage has become a more significant factor.

In 1980, 12% of all births in the UK were outside marriage; by 2004 this had increased to 42%. Though a considerable number of parents were cohabiting at the time of the birth, such relationships tend on average to be of shorter duration than marriage, resulting in single-parent families soon afterwards.

In addition, there has been an increase in births to women not living with the child's father. Thus by 2005, 24% of children lived in a family headed by a lone parent, compared with only 7% in 1972. Children in lone-parent families are more likely to live with their mother than with their father, 9 out of 10 lone parents being mothers. Whereas in the 1970s teenage pregnancies were often followed by 'shot-gun weddings', a young girl is now more likely to have an abortion or look after the baby as a single mother, either at her parents' home, alone in council accommodation or cohabiting with a partner. The majority of teenage conceptions are now out of wedlock.

Problems of terminology

As the word 'single' can sometimes mean unmarried, it is preferable to use the phrase 'lone-parent family' when referring to the whole range of families split by divorce, death or the absence of an unmarried partner. However, even the word 'lone' can be misleading, as the absent parent may be in touch regularly, providing financial and practical support, perhaps looking after the child as part of a weekly arrangement. The lone parent may have moved back to live with his or her parents or share a house with another adult, meaning that children may be cared for by more than just the parents.

Some sociologists, following Murdock's definition of a family as consisting of two parents and their children, prefer the term 'lone-parent household' to 'lone-parent family'. When answering an essay question mentioning, for example, 'single-parent families', it is advisable near the beginning of your response to discuss possible interpretations of the term used.

Have never-married mothers created an underclass?

Never-married mothers share some of the problems of divorced parents, but they are likely, on average, to be younger. They may have fewer qualifications and marketable skills, meaning their earning power is too low to pay for childcare while they work. Unless they receive maintenance from their children's father, they are likely to be dependent on welfare benefits.

American New Right commentator Charles Murray (1994) described UK lone-parent families, especially those resulting from unmarried relationships, as a growing underclass, likening them to the impoverished black-American matrifocal families often associated with crime. However, many sociologists feel this moral panic, generated by such newspapers as *The Sunday Times*, is unjustified.

The term 'underclass' implies a large group sharply divided from the rest of society by different values and lifestyle. Allan and Crow disagreed with this assessment for the following reasons:

- Though it is true that single mothers tend to live in high concentrations in impoverished housing estates, this is because of housing policies and economic necessities, not through choice.
- Only a small minority of single mothers admit to becoming pregnant deliberately, and most knew the limited benefits to which they would be entitled as single parents. Most would prefer to be part of a more conventional couple.
- Fatherless families are blamed by the New Right for juvenile delinquency, because they fail to discipline young boys. However, male physical dominance should not be needed in bringing up teenagers; there is no reason why mothers should not be able to instil appropriate values. Though households may lack responsible male role models, school and family networks may offer plenty of examples.
- The root cause of never-married parenthood is long-term unemployment prospects for working-class males, rather than different values and dependency culture.

Without the constraints generated by commitment to the social order through employment and more traditional family life, including marriage and fatherhood, working class male youths especially are seen as liable to adopt marginalised and anomic life styles…Yet…in areas of high unemployment, the possibility of embracing the traditional masculine role of wage earner and breadwinner are limited, especially for those who do not achieve well educationally, a characteristic feature of being brought up in poverty. Without reasonable prospects of secure employment, they have little to contribute economically to a family. Often the mothers of their children are financially better off controlling their own social security money than claiming as a couple. Thus the absence of employment now and into the foreseeable future does little to encourage stable partnerships or full participation in family life.

G. Allan and G. Crow, *Families, Households and Society* (2001)

How functional are reconstituted families?

Although lone-parent families strike many people as less than ideal arrangements and certainly result in a poorer standard of living, single parents are, on average, younger than married parents, and most find another partner relatively quickly. The resulting arrangement is known as a reconstituted, re-formed, 'blended', 'reconfigured' or 'step' family.

In 2005, almost 9 in 10 stepfamilies consisted of a couple with one or more children from the previous relationship of the woman only, reflecting the tendency for children to stay with their mother following the break-up of a partnership.

Allan and Crow (2001) observed that stepfamilies are difficult to define and therefore to count:

> While stepfamilies certainly embrace those cases where dependent children live with one of their natural parents and a new spouse, they can also include cohabitees; non-residential parents living with new partners; and adult rather than dependent children. A stepfamily may also involve more than one set of stepchildren as well as half siblings born to the new partnership. The picture becomes even more complex with serial cohabitation and/or divorce.

> …It is simplest to focus on the number of dependent children who are living in their main household with a natural parent and a married (or long-term cohabiting) step-parent… there can be no doubt that the numbers have been growing significantly over the last twenty years as divorce, unmarried motherhood and remarriage become more common.
>
> G. Allan and G. Crow, *Families, Households and Society* (2001)

Task 5.4

Read the following extract about stepfamilies and identify some of the problems and benefits that may be experienced in them.

> The National Stepfamily Association (NSA) says 18 million people now live as part of a stepfamily and estimates there will be more stepfamilies than birth families by 2010.

> One in eight British children is now living in a stepfamily. NSA research found each child had a different experience, but many felt excluded from decisions about their future and wanted to feel someone was listening to them. Some saw the experience of being part of a larger family as positive, meaning they had more people to support them, but many felt powerless. Adults and child-guidance professionals need to make it easier for children to talk about their experiences.

> Liz and Patrick Bond have six children between them. Liz had two daughters before she met Patrick and Patrick had three sons. The couple also have a child together. Patrick said it was difficult adjusting to different styles of parenting.

> 'I have been on my own for six years and we were more like a commando unit than a family. I used to shout a lot at the boys, but when I did it to the girls they just crumbled.'

> Liz also had problems. 'You do not love someone else's children in the way you love your own. Being a mother in the same house where you are being a mother to your own children, when you do not have the same natural motherly feelings is very difficult.'

The children say they have had to make adaptations. One said she had been the eldest in her family and could boss her sister around, but in the new family she got bossed around a lot.

But there are positive things about their birth parents' divorce. One said that because she saw each one separately, she had more time with them. 'And it is like having an extra dad,' she added.

Adapted from 'UK Life in a Step Family' BBC online, 24 June 1999

http://news.bbc.co.uk/1/hi/uk/377214.stm

Allan and Crow observed that 'the dynamics of stepfamilies have the potential to become particularly complicated', and many people find themselves unprepared for the challenge. Before the twentieth century, stepfamilies arose most frequently after the death of a natural parent, whereas nowadays the absent parent is usually still alive and often wishes to maintain contact with the children. This more complex situation creates divided loyalties for young people between the step- and natural parents; it can be practically difficult dividing their time between two households, and there may be wrangling between the natural parents about financial support and access. The relatives of the absent parent may also wish for continued contact. Some children enjoy maintaining relationships with old and new sets of caring kin, finding it beneficial, but in other stepfamilies there can be bitterness, as rival adults are played off against each other and angry parents try to reduce access.

Allan and Crow commented that it is difficult for a stepfamily to attain the same sense of unity as a 'natural family' that has acquired a home together, given birth to children and been involved in their upbringing from the start. In contrast, though a new couple coming together may wish to create a similar model for their stepfamily, they bring a history to the relationship and at least one child who has not been socialised by one of the parents. They will have less time and intimacy to forge their own relationship because of the presence of the child, who may resent losing the natural parent's undivided attention. There may be additional rivalries if both adults bring children into the household or if they decide to have children together.

Stepfathers in particular have difficulty asserting discipline over children who are not their own. They are generally expected to maintain order in the household but may be regarded as outsiders by their stepchildren, who might instead appeal to the authority of their mother or natural father. Mothers may feel torn between wishing to support their new partner and providing comfort to their children. The stepfather with no children of his own may have no experience of dealing with children, and tensions may arise if he implies that the children's bad behaviour is attributable to the way they have been brought up so far.

Stepmothers acquire an even more challenging role, as it is still customary for women to take prime responsibility for daily childcare, including emotional support. Everyone is aware that the stepparent may lack the love bond with a child that usually results from childbirth and early nurturing. Responsibility for the child has been acquired as a side effect of the relationship with the adult partner, and neither the stepparent nor the child has chosen each other. This makes the stepmother–child relationship extremely delicate and partly explains why most children stay with their natural mothers when families break up. Stepchildren tend to leave home at an earlier age than children living with two natural parents, a likely indicator of the additional tensions experienced.

Task 5.5

Read the four points below and discuss the questions that relate to them.

(1) The amount of research into stepfamilies is now increasing in the UK and the USA, but most of it so far has been into the experiences of the adults involved.

(2) What little research there has been into children's experiences has tended to come from asking parents about their children's wellbeing and adaptation.

(3) Research is needed into relationships between stepsiblings and half-siblings within a household.

(4) We know little about the role of grandparents in stepfamilies.

- Discuss why you think most research so far has focused on the experiences of parents.
- What would be the benefits and problems of asking children about their experiences of stepfamilies?
- If government funding were available for only one research project, either point 3 or point 4, which would you prioritise and why?

The Exeter study of family breakdown

The Exeter Family Study: Family Breakdown and Its Impact on Children (Monica Cockett and John Tripp, 1994) compared the experiences of children living in different family groups:

- **intact families** (where the child lived with both biological parents), with and without reported marital problems

- **re-ordered families** following the departure of one parent since the child's birth. These were of three types:
  - **lone-parent families** resulting from divorce or separation
  - **stepfamilies**, where the biological parent with whom the child was living had remarried or was cohabiting with a new partner for the first time
  - **re-disrupted families**, where the resident parent's second or subsequent partnerships had broken down

The extensive study carried out in 1991–92 involved social workers conducting long, confidential interviews with children and their parents, the collection of further data from their schools and family doctors, and the use of a self-esteem test. Factors such as social class and mother's education were held constant when making comparisons.

The results were that children in re-ordered families and their parents more often reported difficulties than those in intact families. These included health problems, especially psychosomatic disorders (medical problems with psychological causes), friendship difficulties, needing extra help at school, suffering from low self-esteem and describing themselves as unhappy.

The considerable differences in economic wellbeing between lone-parent families and first-time stepfamilies seemed to have little impact on the children's happiness. In contrast, children from the re-disrupted families were far more likely than those in the other two re-ordered groups to describe themselves as 'often unhappy' or 'miserable'. This confirms findings from US studies that children who have undergone multiple disruptions suffer more severe problems than those who have to cope once with such a situation. This is perhaps because the parents expect the child to cope better when the situation is repeated and fail to recognise the problems being experienced.

In contrast with the findings of some other studies, children living in intact families where there was discord between the parents still had higher self-esteem and better psychological health than those in re-ordered families. However, they had lower self-esteem and worse psychological health than those in intact families *without* discord. Children in re-ordered families who could remember violence between their parents still expressed confused feelings of missing their absent fathers. Not all had been exposed to violence themselves, and even where they *had* been they expressed mixed feelings.

The study concluded that, though economic problems and parental conflict have adverse effects on children, their happiness, health and educational progress are affected more seriously by family breakdown leading to the departure of a parent from the home. The loss of a second parent figure is associated with much poorer outcomes for the child.

Summary

- Aspects of postmodern society such as secularisation, individualism and emphasis on romantic love may be responsible for the decline of the 'cereal packet family'.
- People now marry later; many prefer cohabitation before or instead of marriage.
- Unhappy couples feel less obliged to stay together than in the past. Though obtaining a divorce is easier, the effects are still difficult to cope with for all concerned.
- Many couples delay having children and have smaller families, while childbirth outside marriage is increasingly common. Opinions vary as to whether never-married mothers constitute an underclass.
- Living in stepfamilies can cause a variety of difficulties for both adults and children, though some children welcome access to new kin.
- The Exeter study identified significant differences in wellbeing between children from intact families and those from re-ordered families, especially those subject to multiple disruption.

Task 5.6

Plan an answer to the following essay question:

Examine reasons for changes in patterns of marriage, cohabitation and divorce since 1970. (20 marks)

Guidance

Note the timescale of the question. Making comparisons with the Victorian family would be inappropriate.

Plan separate sections on:

- marriage, including later marriage and remarriage after divorce
- cohabitation; this could include childless single people living together, people cohabiting after divorce and cohabiting couples with their dependent children
- increased divorce

The question implies that you need to provide descriptions of the changes in each of the three key areas, but keep these brief.

You may decide to begin by identifying causes that have given rise to all three of the above, such as secularisation and individualism. Then go on to outline the specific causes of each change.

Task 5.6 (continued)

Social policies such as changes in divorce laws need to be researched from Chapter 6 before you complete your plan. Notice that the question does not ask for the effects of these changes, but you could later collect information for such an essay.

To gain marks for knowledge and understanding (AO1), the main skill being tested in this question, ensure that you include details of appropriate legislation, named research and key terminology. For evaluation marks (AO2), discuss alternative views of the most significant reasons for changes. For example, members of the New Right are likely to blame the availability of welfare benefits for encouraging family breakdown, whereas liberals are more likely to emphasise the increased influence of personal choice.

Useful websites

- National Statistics Online: Families
  www.statistics.gov.uk/CCI/nugget.asp?ID=1161
- Fact sheets from Gingerbread, a single-parent family support group
  www.gingerbread.org.uk/information-and-advice/Factsheets.htm
- 'Sociology Stuff' site; follow the diversity links
  www.homestead.com/rouncefield/family.html

Further reading

- Allan, G. and Crow, G. (2001) *Families, Households and Society*, Palgrave.
- Cockett, M. and Tripp, J. (1994) *The Exeter Family Study: Family Breakdown and Its Impact on Children*, University of Exeter Press.
- McRae, S. (ed.) (1999) *Changing Britain: Families and Households in the 1990s*, Oxford University Press.

How have government policies influenced household diversity?

Chapter 5 examined changes in the family, such as increases in divorce, cohabitation and births outside marriage. Some people regret the decline of the conventional family, believing it is the best way to bring up children and that it provides its members with stability, producing a more orderly, law-abiding society. This view of functionalists such as Murdock and Parsons continues to be held among present-day conservative thinkers, who are usually referred to as the 'New Right'. Traditional followers of most major religions also tend to be wary of radical changes to the family, especially the idea of homosexual households.

Sociologists have debated the extent to which changes in the law and social policies encourage people to change their family behaviour.

Has legislation influenced the divorce rate?

Task 6.1

Look at the graph that follows and identify the period when the increase in the divorce rate was most striking. What do you know about the Divorce Law Reform Act that occurred around that time? How do you think it differed from divorce laws in earlier times?

Task 6.1 (continued)

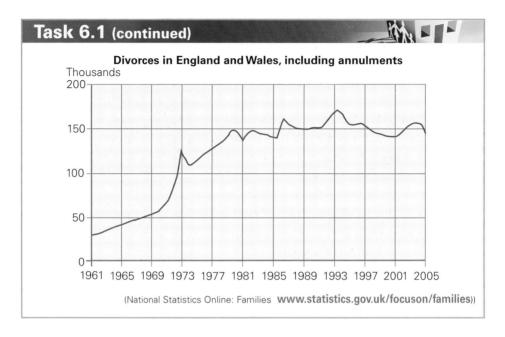

Divorces in England and Wales, including annulments

Thousands

(National Statistics Online: Families **www.statistics.gov.uk/focuson/families**))

A brief history of divorce legislation

Divorce has only been possible for ordinary people for about a century and a half. Before that, people had to pay for a private Act of Parliament to grant them a divorce, so few men and only four women achieved divorces that way. Although according to statistics marriage seemed a more stable institution than nowadays, this was not necessarily the case. Though they were unable to divorce, unhappy couples often lived apart, so their 'empty-shell marriages' existed only on paper. They were unable to forge new relationships, except through committing bigamy or enduring the stigma of cohabitation. William Shakespeare is a famous example of someone who lived apart from his wife for many years, and Victorian novels by Thomas Hardy, Charles Dickens and Charlotte Brontë lament the fate of characters unable to release themselves from marriages to partners who were adulterous, drug addicts or insane. This needs to be taken into account in any discussion of the decline in family life.

- The **Matrimonial Causes Act 1857** made divorce available through the law courts, although the Act was weighted in favour of men. A husband only had to prove that his wife had committed adultery, but a woman had to prove adultery plus either desertion for 2 years, incest, bigamy, sodomy, bestiality, rape or cruelty. The wife's adultery was deemed a more serious matrimonial offence than the husband's, as it risked his property being passed down to children who were not his. However, by the time of this Act a deserted wife could retain her own earnings and property.

- The **Matrimonial Causes Act 1923** gave women equal rights with men on the grounds they could cite for divorce, though proof of the matrimonial offence was still needed.
- The **Matrimonial Causes Act 1937** added other grounds for divorce, such as being of unsound mind, having a communicable venereal disease at the time of marriage or refusing to consummate the marriage.
- The **Legal Aid and Advice Act 1949** enabled poorer people to receive financial assistance to pay divorce solicitors and court costs.
- The **Divorce Reform Act 1969** (in effect from 1971) reflected a change in attitudes: irretrievable breakdown of marriage was now regarded as sufficient grounds for divorce. Before this time, an unhappily married spouse sometimes had to enact a witnessed act of apparent adultery with an obliging friend, simply to provide evidence for the court. Now neither partner needed

Charlotte Brontë's Jane Eyre laments the fate of Mr Rochester, who is unable to release himself from his marriage to an insane partner

to be found at fault, as separation for 2 years was sufficient grounds if both partners agreed, or separation for 5 years if one contested the divorce. Alternatively, unreasonable behaviour or adultery could be cited as evidence for irretrievable breakdown.

Did divorce legislation reflect or encourage the desire to divorce?

It is clear from the graph in Task 6.1 that the divorce rate was already increasing quite quickly in the 1960s, but that it rose dramatically after 1971, partly in response to the new law. Those in unhappy relationships have sometimes had to await appropriate legislation, resulting in a 'dam effect' of potential applicants that may be released in a huge surge once the law comes into effect. This gives the impression for a few years that the law has caused more dramatic changes than is really the case.

In the late 1960s, the government was reluctant to encourage divorce but was sympathetic towards those whose marriages had already broken down. Likewise, the Church of England opposed change on moral grounds but was anxious not to seem out of touch with the times. It is debatable whether some couples would have tried harder to repair their marriages if the legislation had been different.

How has the welfare state influenced the family?

Before the Second World War, the UK lacked a coherent system for supporting the needs of families and the poor, as some people were insured through their work and others had to depend on help from charities, local authorities, friends or relatives. During the years 1945–50, the Labour government developed the welfare state, a comprehensive network of support 'from the cradle to the grave'. Despite some changes, the scheme continues to this day.

The social security system provides financial support for people during vulnerable periods of their lives. People in work pay into the national insurance scheme, and in return they are eligible for benefits such as maternity benefit, sickness benefit and retirement pension. Those who have been unable to contribute to the scheme may still be eligible for income support or a basic retirement pension, and all families can claim child benefit. In addition, there are free school meals, winter fuel allowances for the elderly, rent allowances and other grants for specific needs.

Free services allow everyone to access medical treatment, secondary education and decent housing, regardless of income. The elderly and disabled are provided with help in their homes, such as 'meals on wheels' and chiropody services. Though the National Health Service is no longer entirely free, as dental and prescription charges have been introduced, it has extended its scope in other ways, for example by offering free contraception since 1974.

Why do more people live alone?

The proportion of one-person households in the UK increased by 11% between 1971 and 2001, though it has since remained stable at 29%. The increase in divorce and separation is one reason for the rise, which caused housing shortages in many parts of the country, affecting local planning and provision of supporting services. Another important factor is greater independence of young single people, who are less likely to live with their parents until they find a partner (compare the young woman in Helen Fielding's *Bridget Jones's Diary* with any Jane Austen heroine to support this point). To what extent could the provisions of the welfare state also be responsible?

Task 6.2

Examine the figure below. Suggest reasons for the proportions of people of each gender living alone at different ages. Consider any possible links with the benefits and services provided by the welfare state.

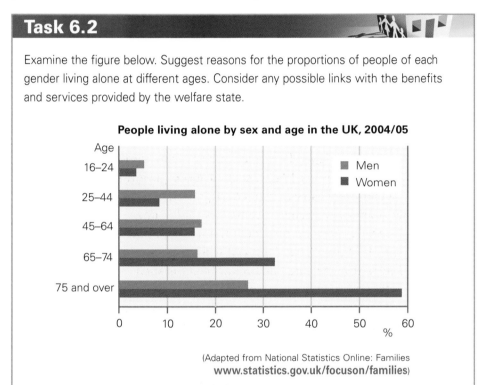

People living alone by sex and age in the UK, 2004/05

(Adapted from National Statistics Online: Families
www.statistics.gov.uk/focuson/families)

Guidance

On average, men still earn more per hour than women, so men of working age can more easily afford a rent or mortgage alone. This may explain why in 2004/05, men living alone were more likely than women to be single, while women living alone were more likely to be divorced or widowed.

In the post-retirement age groups, there were over three times as many widows as widowers in the population in 2004/05, as women tend to live longer than men. The National Health Service has contributed to the longevity and improved health of the elderly, who can afford to live independently because they receive pensions and, in some cases, help towards the cost of rent and winter fuel. The frail elderly may still live alone with the support of the meals-on-wheels service and carers who call several times a day to help them dress and wash. Government policy currently favours such care in the community over residential care, as it preserves people's independence and dignity.

How have social policies affected birth rates?

Family size

How many children people have is a matter of personal choice, but it can be influenced by financial incentives or penalties. Whether contraception and abortion are legally available reflects not only the official religious values of a nation but also its population requirements. In Romania under President Ceauş escu, there were tax incentives to marry early and contraception was unavailable. This was in order to swell the birth rate, but it had the adverse effect of forcing poorer couples to abandon unwanted babies to orphanages. France has generous family allowances for third and subsequent children in order to boost the population. In contrast, China wishes to reduce its population, so couples producing more than one child suffer financial penalties and abortion is recommended instead, resulting in the shortfall of girls described in Chapter 2.

Luckily, the UK has no such extreme policies, though it could be argued that the decreasing amount of child benefit after the first child is a disincentive to have larger families. Practicalities, such as house size and the expense of educating children when so many stay at school beyond the minimum age, are other reasons to limit family size. Equal pay and anti-discrimination legislation have encouraged more women to cut short their childbearing years to return to work, and the legal availability of abortion (in specific circumstances) and free contraception make family limitation achievable.

The provision of free or subsidised nurseries is a significant factor that may influence women's decisions on family size and whether to undertake paid work. During both world wars, extra nurseries were set up to encourage women to join the workforce, but when the men returned from the forces, many were closed. This reflected the view at that time that men should be the main breadwinners.

The availability of nursery care now depends on area. State nursery schools are funded by local authorities and are therefore free. Community pre-schools are run on a non-profit basis, and so charge low fees, whereas privately run nursery schools charge more. Three- and four-year-olds are entitled to free half-day tuition, but this is inadequate for parents in full-time work. Working parents on low incomes receive some help with childcare costs through the child tax credit and working tax credit.

The provision of pre-school education in day-care centres varies greatly around the world, significantly influencing mothers' ability to work and decisions on family size. For example, in Sweden it is available for 37% of children, in Canada for 15% and in Nicaragua for less than 1%.

Illegitimate births

In the UK, the recent steep increase in births to single teenage mothers has been of considerable concern to some policy makers. Members of the New Right, such as the conservative MP John Redwood and US commentator Charles Murray, have argued that the availability of income support and council flats to unmarried mothers has encouraged illegitimate births. The counter-argument of Graham and Crow — that few girls make the conscious decision to become single parents — was discussed in Chapter 5. However, fears that state benefits to single mothers might be encouraging irresponsible fathering and desertion led to the creation of a controversial new agency: the Child Support Agency.

The Child Support Agency

In 1993, the Child Support Agency was established to ensure that parents, usually fathers, pay maintenance for children with whom they no longer live. Though the aims were ostensibly moral (to discourage irresponsible fathering and desertion), critics claimed that reducing the state-benefit bill was the main motivation.

After the agency was set up, about 30% of non-resident parents were persuaded to contribute to their children's maintenance, while unsupported lone parents continued on state benefits. The agency was criticised for penalising cooperative parents, demanding additional payments from those already paying some maintenance instead of pursuing recalcitrant parents who refused to pay anything at all. The flat rate of 30% of fathers' net income for maintenance caused some who had subsequently set up new families enormous hardship, even leading to suicide. Mothers unwilling to contact former partners risked losing benefits, and CSA intervention created acrimony between parents who had previously been cooperating amicably about access to children.

From 2008, the Child Support Agency will be replaced by the Child Maintenance and Enforcement Commission, a body with greater powers to pursue defaulters. Proposals include making it compulsory to have the father's name recorded on the birth certificate to help future enforcement, collecting payments compulsorily from wages, imposing curfews, confiscating passports and 'naming and shaming' the uncooperative who have been taken to court.

Despite the relative weakness of the Child Support Agency, it did at least establish the moral principle that absent fathers should take financial responsibility for their own children. Though maintenance payments might be no higher than the state benefits withdrawn as a consequence, unlike income support they were not affected by the recipient's earnings. This encouraged lone mothers to work, and if they worked over 16 hours per week they might also be entitled to tax credits and financial help with the cost of childcare. However, even this measure is controversial. While the Labour government is keen on 'welfare to work', encouraging the unemployed to gain work experience so they are no longer so dependent and socially excluded, others argue that single parents would be better engaged at home socialising their children. The findings of the Exeter study (Chapter 5) seemed to suggest that family poverty was of less importance to children than the presence of parents.

Task 6.3

Read the passage below and answer the questions that follow.

The perfect recipe for a prosperous marriage: split up

A newly married couple who went to a job centre for advice on benefits were told by a civil servant they would be better off if they split up.

The Fensomes, who have six children between them from previous relationships, had gone to Dunstable job centre to inquire about the benefits they would be entitled to as a married couple.

The Fensomes were so amazed by the advice that they went straight to the surgery of their local Conservative MP. He said government advisers had no right to comment on people's private lives and that the intervention flew in the face of government efforts to encourage family life.

The Fensomes have been a couple for three and a half years but did not live together until their marriage. Mr Fensome was on incapacity benefit until recently and they also get child benefits. Technically, they could be better off if they split because Mrs Fensome would be entitled to lone-parent benefits and a higher level of income support.

A couple get £90.10 a week in income support and single people get £57.45. The latter also get a higher rate of child support and dependent children and young person's benefit. They could be entitled, too, to a slightly higher rate of job seeker's allowance and council tax benefit.

A Department of Work and Pensions spokeswoman said: 'It is true there are good reasons why single people may get a higher total benefit than a couple, and our advisers may be communicating that, but there is no question of Jobcentre Plus policy encouraging people to split up. The rate of benefits for couples reflects the lower costs of sharing living expenses.'

Adapted from an article by Marie Woolf in the *Independent on Sunday*, 26 November 2006

Task 6.3 (continued)

(1) With regard to benefits, to what extent does the situation described in the extract suggest that government policies discourage two-parent families?

(2) How could it be argued that paying proportionately more to adults living alone than to a couple is based on practical rather than moral considerations?

(3) The basic retirement pension for a couple is considerably less than twice the value of the pension for an elderly person living alone. Would it be logical to expect elderly married couples to split up as a result?

Benefits and rights of cohabitees

Even though cohabitation is also sometimes known as 'common-law marriage', this is a meaningless term, as heterosexual couples that cohabit currently have few statutory rights. They are doubly disadvantaged, as their income and assets are counted together for the purpose of claiming social security benefits, meaning, for example, that an unemployed partner cannot claim income support if the other earns a good salary. If one partner dies, the survivor is not entitled to a widow's pension and does not automatically inherit the partner's property. If a couple who have cohabited for years choose to separate, a mother who has sacrificed her career to look after their family can claim maintenance for their children but not for herself, and to claim a fair share of their property is far more difficult than for married couples.

The situation may soon change, in line with increased rights for members of civil (homosexual) partnerships, who now have similar rights to married couples. A change in the law is urgent, as the government estimates that by 2031 almost 4 million couples will be cohabiting. The Law Commission currently investigating the situation is likely to recommend that all cohabitants, whether heterosexual or homosexual, should benefit from intended changes, such as automatic inheritance of the partner's property, providing they have lived together for 2 years.

Task 6.4

(1) Think of one reason why the New Right may object to increased rights for cohabiting couples.

(2) Why might some cohabitees prefer not to have their legal rights extended?

As traditionalists will argue that legislation favouring cohabitees will be a further disincentive to marry, the financial benefits currently being discussed may be less generous than those available to married couples. It is possible that some cohabiting couples will regard the intended legislation as interference by the 'nanny state', especially if they have deliberately avoided marriage in order to retain their independence.

How has social policy influenced homosexual arrangements?

Box 6.1

Elton leads UK gay wedding rush

Pop star Elton John has tied the knot with long-time partner David Furnish, in a civil union ceremony seen as a watershed in the struggle for gay rights.

'It's been a long time coming,' said a fan. 'Admittedly, it's Elton and David's day, but it's the first day that gay couples can engage in civil ceremonies in…England. So I think it's something to celebrate.'

Peter Tatchell, spokesman for the gay and lesbian human rights group OutRage! said the wedding 'would raise the profile of gay love and commitment'.

David Furnish and Elton John

'Their same-sex civil partnership ceremony will be reported all over the world including in countries where news about gay issues is normally never reported. This will give hope to millions of isolated, vulnerable, lesbian and gay people, especially those living in repressive and homophobic countries.'

The new law — passed last year despite some opposition from Parliament's unelected House of Lords — allows civil ceremonies that will give same-sex couples the same social security, tax, pension and inheritance rights as married couples.

However, it has met opposition from some conservative religious groups who say marriage should be restricted to a union between a man and a woman.

Adapted from Aljazeera English archive December 2005
http://english.aljazeera.net/news/archive/archive?ArchiveId=17219

The news story in Box 6.1 about Elton John's civil union with David Furnish is a reminder of one of the changes in household structure that has occurred since Murdock described the universal family as consisting of a male and female and their children. The Civil Partnership Act came into operation on 5 December 2005 and enables a same-sex couple to register as civil partners, receiving many of the same rights as married heterosexual couples as a consequence. The change signals the likely increase in another type of household diversity, characteristic of a postmodern UK.

Homosexual acts between males were prohibited in the Old Testament, and anal intercourse was made illegal in the UK in 1533, to be reinforced by legislation in 1885 prohibiting all male homosexual acts. It was not until 1967 that private sexual acts were permitted between two consenting males over the age of 21 in England and Wales. Lesbian acts have never been illegal in the UK, but publications dealing with the matter were often considered obscene. For example, Radclyffe Hall's novel *The Well of Loneliness* (1928) about a lesbian couple was declared obscene and banned until 1949. During the second wave feminist movement of the 1970s, a considerable number of books were published promoting lesbianism as a preferred alternative to male oppression, especially in the USA.

After 1967, UK gay-rights organisations campaigned for the age of consent to be reduced to 16, the same as for heterosexuals. However, homosexuality was still regarded as more deviant and not to be encouraged, so a compromise was reached at the age of 18 in 1994. Eventually, by the Sexual Offences Amendment Act of 2000, the age of consent was reduced to 16. This now applies in England, Scotland and Wales, but the age of consent for both sexes is 17 in Northern Ireland, perhaps reflecting the province's stronger religious values.

Task 6.5

Consult the Wikipedia website to learn about homosexual laws around the world: http://en.wikipedia.org/wiki/Homosexuality_laws_of_the_world.

- In which countries is homosexuality illegal? Which ones have life imprisonment and death penalties?
- Which countries have laws against homophobia?
- Is there any relationship between the laws on homosexuality and the dominant religion of the country?

Click on the small map of Europe to see which countries permit same-sex marriages or civil unions.

It is also interesting to compare laws on lesbian, gay and transgendered adoption around the world: http://en.wikipedia.org/wiki/LGBT_adoption.

These exercises will help you to understand the huge impact that social policies and laws have on household arrangements.

The UK government's commitment to gay rights is underlined by a series of recent measures:

- **Paternity leave**. From April 2003, a new right to 2 weeks' paid paternity leave was fully introduced, following the provisions in the Employment Act 2002. This is available to a parent who has responsibility for the upbringing of the child, including a mother's or adopter's same-sex partner.
- **Adoption**. The government's objective is to increase the opportunities for vulnerable children to be adopted and grow up as part of a loving, stable and permanent family. The Adoption and Children Act 2002, which was implemented on 30 December 2005, enables same-sex couples (and unmarried heterosexual couples) to apply to adopt a child jointly.

The Adoption of Children Act 2002 enables same-sex couples to apply to adopt a child jointly

- **Commission for Equality and Human Rights**. This new organisation was created in 2006, amalgamating existing organisations dedicated to racial equality, disability rights and equal opportunities. In addition, it has responsibilities for rights in relation to age, sexual orientation and religion and will ensure that organisations such as unions and citizens' advice bureaux have the correct training to advise people on these rights.
- **White Paper proposal to change fertility treatment laws**. Under proposals to update the law on assisted conception and embryo research, fertility clinics will no longer be able to deny treatment to lesbians and single mothers. In the past, they have been required to consider the need for a father when deciding to offer treatment. The new plan is that if same-sex couples are using IVF to conceive, both should be legally recognised as parents. It also recommends extending parental rights to a partner who is not the biological parent of a child conceived with donor eggs and sperm (source: the *Guardian*, 14 December 2006).

How diverse are households in the UK and elsewhere?

So far our discussion has focused on structural or organisational diversity, examining the make-up of family groups in terms of the number of parents, grandparents, partners and children and their roles. Some sociologists have been interested by other types of variety, relating to:

- ethnic group
- social class
- locality

- nation
- cohort
- life course

Ethnic group

Families with different religious beliefs or cultural origins are likely to have varying lifestyles.

Relationships between the generations

Sharon Beishon, Tariq Modood and Satnam Virdee (1998) interviewed a sample of almost 100 ethnic minority members and white people living in London, finding that most of the Pakistanis and Bangladeshis believed that parents and their adult children should live together, with married sons moving their wives into the household.

> This was an ideal solution for living, which fostered deep and meaningful relationships, helped pass on cultural practices and ensured that the family would function as a mutually rewarding support system.
>
> S. Beishon, T. Modood and S. Virdee, *Ethnic Minority Families* (1998)

Nearly a quarter of the interviewees were living in an extended family with in-laws, siblings or cousins, and some others would like to have done so if large enough accommodation had been available. Typically in such families, married women were not employed, income was held jointly and managed by the eldest male; marriages were arranged but with a say in the choice of spouse.

In contrast, Indian and African Asians tended to believe that married children should set up home on their own, but be near enough to support parents when necessary. In practice, the generations were more likely to move back under the same roof as the parents got older. Arranged marriages were becoming less common among younger generations of Sikhs, Hindus and African-Asians.

In contrast with whites and African-Caribbeans:

...all unmarried children of South Asian parents, regardless of their age, were expected to live with parents, who felt that they might become assimilated into a British culture, away from ethno-religious values and traditions. This would be a source of shame and anxiety.

S. Beishon, T. Modood and S. Virdee, *Ethnic Minority Families* (1998)

Beishon's interviews were semi-structured, seeking people's opinions and values. The results were compared with statistics collected from a larger study of 8,000 minority and white respondents, the Fourth National Survey of Ethnic Minorities (1994). This revealed a disparity between the family lifestyles people say they prefer and the reality. Thus African-Caribbeans told Beishon that they did not want their parents living with them, valuing their own space and privacy, but the larger survey found a third of African-Caribbean elders living with their children.

Sexual relationships

South Asians perceived cohabitation as a loose arrangement in which men were likely to abandon women and children. They considered illegitimacy shameful, while marriage was highly valued as a stable environment for children and a deep commitment for partners.

In contrast, many single African-Caribbeans wanted to be married but viewed cohabitation as a practical first step. They viewed the level of commitment between partners as more important than legal arrangements, the majority stating that there was little difference between cohabitation and marriage, an opinion echoed by many of the whites interviewed. The Fourth National Survey of Ethnic Minorities (1994) showed the realisation of such attitudes, with 18% of African-Caribbean couples cohabiting, compared with 11% of whites and between 2% and 4% for Asian groups. Marriage may be less customary among African-Caribbeans than among whites because it was outlawed during slavery. However, the West Indian houseyard system provided practical and financial support for the unmarried mother not so easily found in the urban UK.

Beishon found African-Caribbeans and whites tolerant of divorce in a whole range of circumstances, whereas south Asians found it unacceptable. These attitudes are reflected in recent statistics. Of the groups compared in the UK census for 2001, Hindus and Sikhs are the least likely to be divorced, separated or remarried. This pattern was the same across most age groups. For example, among 45- to 54-year-olds, 10% of Sikhs and 11% of Hindus who had ever been married described their current marital status as divorced, separated or remarried. This compares with 17% of Muslims, 34% of Christians and 43% of those with no religion in the same age group (National Statistics Online).

Despite the UK frequently being described as multicultural, inter-ethnic marriages form only 2%, according to the 2001 census for England and Wales.

(Ethnic backgrounds were defined broadly as white, mixed, Asian, black, Chinese, or other ethnic group.) The most common inter-ethnic marriages were:

- between white and mixed-race people — 26% of all inter-ethnic marriages
- between a white person and someone describing their ethnic group as 'other' (15%)
- white and black African-Caribbean marriages (12%)
- white and Indian marriages (11%)

People from south Asian backgrounds were the least likely of the minority ethnic groups to be married to someone from a different ethnic group, probably because of religious as well as cultural differences from the other groups. Beishon's interviews confirmed a reluctance to contemplate mixed-ethnicity partnerships:

> Marriage is an important indicator of the distinctiveness of different ethnic identities. There was virtually no sign that the various minorities saw each other as forming a common pool from which to select non-white partners.
>
> S. Beishon, T. Modood and S. Virdee, *Ethnic Minority Families* (1998)

Despite the UK frequently being described as multicultural, inter-ethnic marriages form only 2%, according to the 2001 census for England and Wales

Social classs

In *Underclass: the Crisis Deepens* (1994), Charles Murray predicted a return to more traditional family values among the upper middle class (the 'New Victorians'), contrasting this with family decline among the working class ('New Rabble'):

> Illegitimacy in the lower classes will continue to rise and, inevitably, life in lower class communities will continue to degenerate — more crime, more widespread drug and alcohol addiction, fewer marriages, more dropout from work, more homelessness, more child neglect, fewer young people pulling themselves out of the slums, more young people tumbling in.
>
> Charles Murray, *Underclass: the Crisis Deepens* (1994)

This extreme right-wing view, which typically links deviance with family structures, makes an exaggerated contrast between classes compared with other research. Kathleen Kiernan and Valerie Estaugh's detailed study *Cohabitation: Extra-Marital Childbearing and Social Policy* (1993) distinguished between three major groups of cohabitees. They found few socioeconomic differences between childless cohabitants and their childless married contemporaries, predicting that living together before marrying will become the norm for the young of all classes, similar to couples in the past becoming engaged. They also noted that all social groups were represented among post-marital cohabitants, half of whom had children from previous marriages. Only a third group of never-married cohabitants with children were relatively disadvantaged, being more likely than married-couple families to be living in council accommodation with the father unemployed or in a lower paid occupation.

Locality

David Eversley and Lucy Bonnerjea (1982) suggested that distinctive types of families predominate according to region:

- The 'sun belt' — the affluent south of England — attracts two-parent upwardly mobile families.
- The 'geriatric wards' — coastal areas of England and Wales — have a dispro-portionate number of elderly people.
- Older declining industrial areas have traditional families resembling Willmott and Young's Stage 2 type.
- Newly declining areas, such as the Midlands, have more diverse patterns, including recent arrivals without family support.
- Inner-city areas have the cheapest housing, attracting disadvantaged groups including recent immigrants, lone parents and students.
- Truly rural areas, as opposed to commuter villages, may have family-based farms.

It could be added that many prosperous UK couples buy property in western Europe on retirement, often living there during the winter months.

Nation

As we have seen, family structures outside the UK vary enormously, particularly when social policies influence family size and laws prohibit homosexuality or permit polygamy.

One experiment in living, popular in Denmark and parts of the USA, is co-housing, described by John Scanzoni in *Designing Families: The Search for Self and Community in the Information Age* (2000). This involves families, singles and others living in their own homes within a small cooperative community, where the members interchange emotional support, childcare and help with the elderly much as an extended family would.

Cohort

Different generations are influenced by the predominant values of their formative years. Hence, those who grew up in the 1970s are more likely to favour cohabitation and egalitarian family roles than older people. However, their family choices are not fully predictable, as life courses vary so much.

Life course

The term 'life course' refers to the narrative of a person's life, the stages through which people of similar ages typically pass, such as:

- birth and childhood in the family of origin
- leaving home and single adulthood
- marriage without children
- birth of children, a new nuclear family
- middle age, children leave home
- old age, living alone when the partner dies

Kenneth Roberts (1995) argued that the life course is de-standardised now compared with in the past. In older communities, the majority of young people stayed in the locality to enter traditional occupations, so members of a peer group tended to marry and have children at roughly the same time. Nowadays, people's lives are likely to diverge because of changes in society. The conventional stages may be approached in a different order, such as having children before marriage or completing a university course in middle age. Reasons for this de-standardisation include the following:

- There is a wider variety of educational and training options and jobs.
- There is greater geographical and social mobility, especially with the increase in university education. Unmarried young people are less likely to live with their parents.
- Changes in technology and the economy mean fewer 'jobs for life'. People may have to retire early or change careers and locality.
- Women's options are more varied in terms of work and family planning.
- Less cohesive neighbourhoods tolerate a wider variety of lifestyles, including cohabitation and homosexuality.
- Marriages are less likely to be for life. Many people start second families.

Is the family in decline?

The New Right and various religious groups deplore 'the death of the family'. However, despite the changes in family structure and lifestyle catalogued above, it is useful to be reminded of several counter-examples:

- Robert Chester (1985) and others since have argued that the family is still the most popular way to live. If people are counted instead of households, over half are living in nuclear-family households at any one time. Others have done so in the past and will do so in the future. Chester called the modern family neo-conventional, indicating that the only difference from the 'cereal packet family' is that mothers are more likely to be wage earners.

- Criminologist Joan McCord (1982) followed the criminal careers of US males first observed in the 1940s. She found offenders were nearly twice as common from intact homes where the parents were in conflict as those raised in one-parent families by an affectionate mother. The quality of home life was more crucial than the number of parents.

- Most illegitimate births are registered in the father's name as well as the mother's, suggesting the child is likely to have at least *some* contact with the father. About three-quarters of such joint-registered births show the parents living at the same address. Many may eventually marry or at least maintain a stable relationship while the child is maturing.

- Even though divorce has increased, children may be co-parented or remain in contact with the absent partner. Groups such as Fathers 4 Justice demonstrate male enthusiasm to have regular contact with their children from failed partnerships.

- The majority of those who divorce before the age of 35 remarry within 10 years, though more men do so than women. A recent estimate suggested the mean length of time spent as a lone parent is a little over 5 years (Rowlingson and McKay, 1998). Therefore, the children of broken marriages often gain step-parents within a few years, benefiting from the support of two adults.

- The decision to divorce then remarry has been interpreted by some to suggest that people seek higher standards in their partnerships than those in the past, who simply endured unhappy marriages.

Summary

- Divorce legislation has undoubtedly influenced the divorce rate, though new legislation often reflects existing changes in behaviour and attitudes.
- The welfare state's benefits and services have encouraged many family changes, for example allowing the elderly and single mothers to cope alone, though New Right critics claim welfare payments encourage illegitimacy.
- The Child Support Agency was a controversial attempt to combat irresponsible parenting.
- Cohabiting couples lack some of the rights of married couples, whereas civil partnerships and laws enabling homosexuals to adopt children are likely to increase household diversity.

- There are many types of family diversity in the modern UK and people's life courses are no longer predictable. However, there is some evidence to counteract the view that the family is in decline.

Task 6.6

Read the extract below and then answer the question that follows.

Conservatives back return to Victorian values

The Conservatives are to launch a crusade for personal morality to try to halt a breakdown in traditional family values. They claim the rise in cohabitation and single parenthood is unleashing a social and economic crisis. In an appeal to grassroots supporters, the party will put the promotion of marriage back at the heart of its agenda, warning of dire consequences if more couples are not encouraged to wed.

The Breakdown Britain report commissioned by David Cameron, the Tory leader, claims the breakdown of the family is driving boys into the arms of street gangs at an annual cost to the country of more than £20 billion. The report is likely to be seized on by Labour as evidence that Tory social attitudes have not changed under Cameron and that the party continues to disapprove of many modern families.

The report of the Social Justice Policy Group gives an insight into the possible elements of the party's next election manifesto. It warns that family breakdown, drug and alcohol addiction, welfare dependency and educational failure have created an underclass mired in misery and 'cut off from much of mainstream society'. The burgeoning underclass also 'threatens the wellbeing of middle-class people living in once tranquil neighbourhoods'.

The report suggests that without a radical reappraisal of government policy towards marriage and the family, social tensions will grow, fuelling violent crime.

Adapted from an article by Isabel Oakeshott in *The Sunday Times*,
10 December 2006
www.timesonline.co.uk/article/0,,2087-2496320,00.html

Using material from the article and elsewhere, assess the view that social policies on the family reflect an ideological view of the 'ideal' family type. (20 marks)

Guidance

- In such a question, it is useful to begin by commenting on the article, in order to gain interpretation and application marks (AO2). Identify the Conservative viewpoint as in defence of the 'ideal' family.
- Describing this 'ideal' family as the 'cereal packet' or conventional family will demonstrate knowledge 'from elsewhere' (AO1). Expand on this part of your answer by making links between the ideas in 'Breakdown Britain' and those of New Right commentators such as Charles Murray.

Task 6.6 (continued)

- Remember that the key word 'assess' suggests an alternative view. Many of the social policies outlined in this chapter have supported unconventional households. Discuss several of these, such as benefits to single parents and rights to members of civil partnerships, explaining how they reflect tolerance of diversity as opposed to a traditional family ideology (sometimes known as 'familism'). Legislation since 1997 has reflected New Labour policy, reminding you that it is too sweeping to generalise about UK social policies as they vary with the party in power, even though there is considerable common ground between the current main parties. These last points could be a useful way to conclude your essay, gaining evaluation marks (AO2). AO2 skills are the main requirement of questions beginning with the word 'assess'.

Research

Devise sensitive interviews or questionnaires to see if fellow students of different ethnic backgrounds have similar views on family arrangements to those described by Beishon, Modood and Virdee in 1998. To what extent do younger generations retain traditional attitudes?

Recommended websites

- Women and Equality Unit sections on civil partnerships and on gay and lesbian issues
  www.womenandequalityunit.gov.uk/civilpartnership/index.htm
- 'Introduction to Social Policy', includes useful list of online resources, including international sites
  www2.rgu.ac.uk/publicpolicy/introduction/ukgovt.htm
- 'Tough New Powers on Child Support', BBC article about the Child Maintenance and Enforcement Commission
  http://news.bbc.co.uk/1/hi/uk/6174671.stm

Further reading

- Beishon, S., Modood, T. and Virdee, S. (1998) *Ethnic Minority Families*, Policy Studies Institute.
- Kiernan, K. and Estaugh, V. (1993) *Cohabitation: Extra-marital Childbearing and Social Policy*, Family Policy Studies Centre.
- Murray, C. (1994) *Underclass: the Crisis Deepens*, IEA Health and Welfare Unit in association with *The Sunday Times*.

How have gender and age roles changed in the family?

To what extent have gender roles changed?

Does it seem to you to be implausible that in a so-called 'male-dominated society', a patriarchy, a man is not allowed to be father to his children as he may wish and choose? If you think that men automatically get their own way in all conditions and circumstances of family and professional life in our society, you have to ask yourself why it should be that they so infrequently get what they ask for in the divorce courts.

N. Lyndon, *No More Sex War: The Failures of Feminism* (1992)

Neil Lyndon's passionate remarks, which will be explored more fully in due course, make it clear that there are differing opinions about which sex is currently dominant in UK society. Has feminism made any difference to the roles of the sexes and their relative power, particularly in family matters?

Whether conjugal roles (those of husband and wife) have changed over recent years is an important subject of debate among sociologists. Young and Willmott, in *The Symmetrical Family* (1973), described roles in the Stage-2 family as segregated, with wives mainly responsible for childcare and housework and husbands for financially supporting the family. In the Stage-3 family, they described the roles as joint. Men helped with domestic work and spent more time with their children. Women were often wage earners. This family was more democratic and symmetrical, and the husband has since become known as the new man, i.e. one willing to take on traditionally female roles.

However, Ann Oakley (1974) dismissed Young and Willmott's claim that a husband's once-weekly help with a domestic task constituted significant sharing of responsibilities. In her own study, she found that only 15% of husbands helped with housework to a substantial degree, and only 25% with childcare. Middle-class men participated more in both than working-class respondents.

Graham Allan (1985) criticised Young and Willmott's methodology, pointing out that their sample of couples aged between 30 and 49 excluded younger women with small children, who probably would have spent longer on housework. There appear to be other social factors affecting conjugal role sharing. Roger Jowell (1987) found that older people had more traditional attitudes than the young. Elizabeth Bott (1971) discovered that pre-marriage friendship patterns affected the couples' roles. Those who had belonged to a close-knit circle of friends were less likely to spend so much leisure time or share domestic tasks with their spouse than those whose friends did not know each other.

In the 1970s, research in this area took issue with functionalists such as Parsons, who justified segregated roles because of the assumption that men and women have different natures and aptitudes. Feminists expressed the view that housework is less satisfying than wage labour because it:

- has no contracts, holidays or promotion prospects
- is isolated and has unlimited hours
- is often taken for granted

The view that household gadgets have liberated women is a myth, as higher standards of cleanliness are expected than in previous centuries, and tasks such as ironing are still time-consuming and repetitive.

As more women entered the labour market in the 1980s, researchers became interested in the stresses experienced by dual role or double shift women, whose husbands tolerated their demanding careers, provided they still took responsibility for most of the housework and childcare (or made arrangements themselves for carers and cleaners). Marxist feminists identified double exploitation, by bosses at work and husbands at home.

In response to the suggestion that 'new men' shared some domestic tasks with working wives, Mary Boulton (1983) argued that who takes primary responsibility is more important than who does what. In over 80% of the families she studied, wives took the main responsibility for childcare and where necessary gave it priority over their career or felt guilt when they did not. Along similar lines, Allan (1985) found that, while men were willing to carry out irregular tasks such as household repairs and the more enjoyable aspects of childcare such as trips to the park, their wives were left with the bulk of mundane daily chores.

Jonathan Gershuny (1992) decided to investigate whether men's attitudes towards housework really have changed by comparing hours spent on domestic work in 1974 and 1987. Where wives worked full time, he found a small increase in men's share of cleaning and cooking (more than 20 minutes a day). However, though men appeared to be making some effort, working women still put in over twice as many hours as men, taking paid and domestic work together.

Research by Janet Finch (1989) and Hilary Graham (1990) identified an additional role usually undertaken by women: the responsibility for emotional support and day-to-day organisation of the lives of other family members and kin, creating a **triple shift**.

Task 7.1

Consider the methodological difficulties of asking couples about the amount of household work they do.

- Would you count individual tasks or the amount of time spent?
- Alan Warde in 1988 asked couples who usually did particular tasks and then who last did the tasks. Why do you think he asked both questions?
- What would count as an average day or week?
- Would you rely on respondents' estimates of how long they spent on tasks or ask them to keep a diary? What might the effects be of diary keeping on the validity of results?
- How would you assess people's responsibility for emotional support for family members?

Guidance

This exercise has probably made you aware of why researchers in this field arrive at such varying results (AO2 improving your evaluation skills).

Have power relationships within the family changed?

Besides its more dramatic manifestations, such as domestic violence and child abuse, the distribution of power within the family can be demonstrated by patterns of decision-making and control of finances.

Stephen Edgell's study of decision-making (1980) revealed that, while wives decided what children's clothes and food to buy, husbands chose the car and whether to move house and made major financial decisions. The majority of the middle-class wives interviewed by Edgell viewed it as the man's right to make major decisions, as he was the main breadwinner. Though times are changing, on average women still earn less per hour than men, particularly in older couples; it would be interesting to replicate this study to see if women are more assertive now.

Hilary Graham (1990) found many women had no idea how much their husbands earned. They were given housekeeping money but felt unable to spend money on themselves, whereas their husbands paid major bills then spent the balance as they wished. C. Vogler and J. Pahl (1993) described a similar scenario, relating marital discord to male control of finances. However, David Cheal (2002) believed that about half of couples in the UK pool their incomes in a joint bank account from which either can draw. The discrepancy between his assessment and other researchers' findings underlines the difficulties of obtaining truthful answers on family affairs, especially as many people regard finances as a private matter. Cheal found:

> Whether or not most married couples are actually equally involved in money management and control, many of them want to believe in income pooling as a feature of their relationship…a way of expressing unity in marriage. It involves deliberately ignoring economic differences which exist between most husbands and wives. Pooling first became popular around the time that the ideology of the companionship family emerged.
>
> D. Cheal, *Sociology of Family Life* (2002)

While it appears relatively unusual for married couples in the UK to keep their earnings separate, cohabiting couples frequently manage their finances independently and share bills half and half. If their commitment becomes deeper and more explicit, income pooling is more likely to occur.

How have males responded to feminism?

As females have taken advantage of increasing equal opportunities and become more successful in education and careers, while still being viewed as the central figure within the home, some men have felt their roles diminish. This crisis in masculinity has been particularly associated with young working-class males, whose employment prospects have declined in a post-industrial UK. Susan Faludi's warning in *Backlash: the Undeclared War against Women* (1992), that men would combat feminist influence, has been realised in a number of male pressure groups and books. The UK Men and Fathers' Rights Organisation virulently condemns discrimination against men in many spheres of life, including criminal law, education, health and the family. Fathers 4 Justice has

A campaign by Fathers 4 Justice

conducted highly publicised campaigns to enable fathers to gain freer access to children after parents split up.

In *No More Sex War: the Failures of Feminism* (1992), Neil Lyndon took a different stance, arguing that even though men are now disadvantaged in many spheres, 'movements, banners and marches' will only alienate the sexes. The interests of men and women are inseparable and complementary, not diametrically opposed, so it should be possible to cooperate to improve life for both. Women remain outnumbered in senior posts because they are expected to interrupt their careers for children, whereas men see too little of their children and are viewed as marginal figures in the family. Instead of trying to improve professional day care for children, it would be better to involve fathers more fully:

> If men and women are both, equally, expected to do much less work when their babies are born and during the years of their children's infancies, the professional disadvantages of women disappear…If both men and women are entitled to equal rights of leave from work and all the concessions and encouragements a modern society can provide by way of tax breaks, subsidies…and honours, women would be less frantic in trying to resolve the demands of family and career and, in consequence, men would be allowed to be more attentive and loving fathers.
>
> Neil Lyndon, *No More Sex War: the Failures of Feminism* (1992)

Lyndon suggested that young parents should be given more money to do less work while bringing up their children. Each parent's working week could be cut by half, so that between them they could look after their children full time, providing a more loving environment than a state nursery. (Note the contrast here with kibbutzim and Soviet ideas.) The resulting shortage of labour could be filled by those currently unemployed and by older people such as the postwar generation of 'baby-boomers', who now live longer, healthier lives and do not need to retire in their early sixties. As men became more involved and competent parents, their rights in the event of divorce would be properly recognised, but as the quality of conjugal relationships would undoubtedly be improved by the proposed changes, it is likely that more families would stay intact.

Task 7.2

Discuss Lyndon's proposals.
- Would the proposals help to address the crisis in masculinity?
- Would it be practical to divide and redistribute jobs in the way he suggests?
- What would be the benefits of two parents sharing infant day care?
- What are the different views on the relative merits of professional nursery care and infants staying at home with parents?

While Lyndon wrote mainly about married couples with increasing family diversity, conjugal-role studies are now less relevant to the whole population. Stepfamilies often arrange their finances differently from first-time marrieds, as the absent parent may be contributing to the children's maintenance and may be involved in childcare too. The notion of gendered division of labour is irrelevant to single parents. Some single mothers may see their roles as primarily a carer, managing on maintenance payments or state benefits. Other single mothers and most single fathers may opt for paid work, sharing the childcare role with paid carers or relatives. The division of labour and resources of homosexual and lesbian couples is likely to vary considerably with their degree of commitment and whether they adopt children.

Task 7.3

Plan an answer for the following essay.

Assess the view that the positions of men and women in the family have changed in recent years. (20 marks)

Guidance
- The key word 'assess' should be a reminder to present at least two contrasting arguments (AO2 evaluation skills). 'Recent years' is unlikely to refer back much before the 1970s.

Task 7.3 (continued)

- Clarify that 'positions' refers to relative power, such as decision-making and control of finances, which may reflect earning power and the division of labour within the family (conjugal roles). You could also draw on material from earlier chapters of this book, for example referring to feminist views about 'sexual politics', female exploitation and changes in legal rights, such as the law against marital rape (1991), to show knowledge and understanding (AO1).
- One section of your essay could argue that patriarchy continues, supported by appropriate conjugal role and decision-making studies.
- Another section could provide evidence, particularly from male sources, of perceived male disadvantage and 'the crisis in masculinity', as well as more positive studies showing a more equal division of domestic duties and decision-making between the sexes.
- A short section could point out the growing significance of single-parent and homosexual households.
- Remember to include a conclusion, expressing a final opinion (AO2 evaluation) and incorporating the key terms in the question.

How is childhood socially constructed?

As well as investigating adult roles within the family, sociologists are interested in the status and roles of children and young people. Nowadays, lifestyle depends greatly on age, and there are many age-related laws. Some legislation is designed to protect children from potentially dangerous experiences and substances, implying that they are more vulnerable than adults. Primary school children are expected to play and enjoy life while they can, with whole shops being devoted to their toys, books and outfits. It is assumed that young people are less capable of making rational decisions, so for example 16-year-olds currently cannot vote, nor marry without their parents' permission.

It is not universal to treat children so differently from adults. Despite their biological immaturity, children may carry 'adult' responsibilities in some developing countries. The notion of childhood as a separate state is a social construction, a concept that varies between cultures.

Philippe Aries traced historical changes in attitudes to the young in *Centuries of Childhood* (1962). Medieval pictures showed children playing and working alongside adults, indistinguishable except by size. It was impossible to shelter them from the harsh realities of life because whole families often lived in the same room, and most were not separated from adults by schooling.

Aries identified changing attitudes towards children from the sixteenth century, when the Church became more concerned about safeguarding morals. He described middle-class eighteenth-century couples as coddling their children, distinguishing them from adults by more gentle treatment. The Romantic philosopher Jean-Jacques Rousseau was ahead of his time with his educational treatise *Emile* (1762), which suggested that childish innocence was preferable to adult sophistication. The young should not be forced to accept Christian teaching but be allowed to make up their own minds when old enough.

However, by modern standards, working-class children were exploited at least until the late Victorian period. In 1842, Lord Ashley's Children's Employment Commission revealed that, in the heat of coal mines, men worked naked alongside women stripped to the waist and unsupervised children as young as 6. The resulting Mines Act 1842 forbade the employment underground of children below 10 years of age and women. Likewise, children worked in dangerous and exhausting conditions alongside adults in factories until the Factory Act of 1833 made it illegal for those under 9 to work in textile factories, and limited those aged 9–13 to 8 hours' work a day. Those in their mid-teens were still unprotected until the Factory Act 1847 limited the work of 13- to 18-year-olds to 58 hours a week!

Working-class children were exploited at least until the late Victorian period

In *Songs of Innocence and Experience* (1794), the poet William Blake protested against the use of climbing boys to clean chimneys, an unhealthy and often fatal practice that was not completely outlawed until 1875. It was not unusual for orphans to sleep rough and operate as criminal gangs until 1866, when Dr Thomas Barnardo began to set up schools and orphanages for the destitute of east London. There was nothing to stop adults beating children daily until the Reverend Benjamin Waugh founded the National Society for the Prevention of Cruelty to Children in 1889.

By 1880, education was compulsory, separating children from adults for most of the day. This significantly changed the character of childhood by preventing the young from being significant wage earners and making them instead a source of expense to their parents.

In the next 100 years, social sciences developed a greater understanding of the influences of upbringing and environment on children. The writings of psychiatrist Sigmund Freud (1856–1939) made parents conscious of the possible effects of child-rearing practices. The juvenile justice system acknowledged that child offenders might not be fully responsible for their own actions and needed different treatment from adults. The welfare state stressed the importance and potential vulnerability of the young by making children's allowances available to families, providing free school meals to the needy, school medical and dental checks, child guidance, social worker support and health visitors to check that new mothers knew how to raise their children healthily and safely.

It is so taken for granted in contemporary UK society that children need special care, that any other way of constructing childhood may be difficult to imagine. However, in some other parts of the world children are treated much as they were in previous centuries in the UK. There are many developing countries where children work long hours in dangerous conditions, sleep rough, have little education and marry in their early teens. Worse, children may be exploited as prostitutes and soldiers, and in the poorest circumstances they may be killed, sold or abandoned by their parents. Colin Turnbull's study of the Ik of Northern Uganda (1974) found that parents faced with a food shortage turned children out at about 3 years old to fend for themselves, knowing that most of them would die.

Task 7.4

- Consult the UNICEF site to find out about the Convention on the Rights of the Child, clicking on the 'photo essays' for international examples of children living in different situations.
  www.unicef.org/crc

Task 7.4 (continued)

- Read about the activities and history of the service ChildLine, which was formed in 1986.
  www.childline.org.uk/AboutChildLine.asp
- Find out about the intentions behind recent appointments of Children's Commissioners for England, Scotland and Wales, consulting websites such as the following:
  www.everychildmatters.gov.uk/strategy/childrenscommissioner
  http://news.bbc.co.uk/1/hi/wales/449571.stm
- Why are some people unhappy with the idea of 'child power'?
- Read about the UK Youth Parliament and discuss it with fellow students who have been involved.
  www.ukyouthparliament.org.uk
- Compare the ways childhood and youth are constructed in these different sources.

What are the current concerns about children?

Some researchers are concerned that childhood, as a distinctive period of innocence and carefree activities, is vanishing because of pressures to grow up too fast. In *The Disappearance of Childhood* (1983), Neil Postman blamed television for children behaving more like adults. It is impossible to shield them from the sexual knowledge and violence contained in the electronic media, especially when many children watch unsupervised in their bedrooms, and the effects can be seen in the increasing number of 'adult' crimes they commit and in rising teenage pregnancy. Nowadays, supporters of Postman's view would include the influence of computer games and internet pornography.

Sue Palmer's *Toxic Childhood* (2006) expresses a similar viewpoint. Drawing on interviews with experts in many fields, Palmer, an educational consultant, highlights the recent increase in attention deficit and hyperactivity disorder (ADHD), dyslexia and autism in children in the developed world, as well as high figures for substance abuse, self-harm and attempted suicide. She claims these alarming symptoms of unhappiness and dysfunction are a response to deficits in the following:

- healthy food
- exercise and unstructured play, especially in natural surroundings
- long, regular sleep patterns

- emotional security and stability throughout childhood
- secure childcare arrangements and good role models
- time to interact with family with quality talk
- the gradual encouragement of self-discipline
- positive ethos at pre-school and school
- neighbourhood support

In order to 'detox childhood', Palmer recommends the banning of marketing to pre-teen children and of junk food sales in schools, as well as more control over mobile phone ownership. She claims that both mothers and fathers are too busy working to give children full attention, even dealing with business e-mails and calls, in what should be family time at home. They occupy their children with 'electronic babysitters', such as television and computers, and guiltily give in to their demands for advertised consumer products without making them genuinely happy.

> It doesn't mean stopping our children enjoying TV, computer games or the excitement of the web. It simply means finding a balance between technological fixes and human needs — being warm but firm with ourselves about the extent to which we allow technology to determine our lifestyle. It also means addressing our work-life balance with the same warmth and firmness, and taking an authoritative hold on the way we choose to spend our time.
> S. Palmer, *Toxic Childhood: How the Modern World is Damaging Our Children and What We Can Do About It* (2006)

Along similar lines, Richard Louv's *Last Child in the Woods: Saving Our Children from Nature-Deficit Disorder* (2005) advocates allowing children to spend more time exploring outdoors instead of occupying them with electronic media and consumer goods. Likewise Frank Furedi (*Paranoid Parenting*, 2001) argues that our construction of childhood as an age of vulnerability results in overprotection, so that even play parks have all the potential hazards removed, losing their challenge and excitement. John Hood-Williams (1990) argued that UK parents exercise excessive power over their children, controlling their dress, cleanliness, whereabouts and what they do at particular ages, inhibiting the young through 'age patriarchy'. Perhaps in response to these anxieties, in 2006 the Children's Society began an inquiry into the state of childhood, which received much media attention. The Archbishop of Canterbury, Dr Rowan Williams, endorsed the need to investigate the situation, noting that 1 in 10 children has measurable mental health problems.

Sociologists seem divided about whether childhood is 'disappearing', whether young people grow up too soon or not soon enough. Those who argue that children are given insufficient independence by overprotective parents note that they may not be allowed to walk to school or play in the street, so they develop little traffic sense and become obese. Kenneth Roberts (1995) observed that young people have been dependent on their parents for longer in the last two decades because of extended education, high unemployment and the withdrawal of state benefits for 16- and 17-year-olds. Their continued residence with their natal family may lead to conflict, and 45% of teenagers who leave home do so because of arguments. Yet those who lack family support are more likely to become homeless, jobless and involved in crime. A relatively new phenomenon is graduates returning to live with their parents while they pay off university loans.

On the other hand, there are concerns about childhood loss of innocence, consumerism, increasing educational stress and mental illness, sexual precocity, teenage pregnancies, access to violent media and other adult material and a few high-profile crimes such as rape and murder committed by offenders in their early teens.

These two arguments are not necessarily incompatible, as it may be true that in some behaviour young people are more like adults while being financially dependent on them for longer.

Wherever the truth lies, there are undoubtedly widespread concerns about child health, both physical and mental, and aspects of deviance such as delinquency and drug taking, justifying the proposed inquiry into the state of childhood. As most of today's young people will eventually become parents, it is clear that the future of the family and the nature of society as a whole depend on them.

Summary

- Conjugal-role studies suggest women still devote more hours to housework and childcare than men and take primary responsibility for emotional support too.
- However, men are helping more, particularly with childcare.
- There is conflicting evidence about gender roles in decision-making and control of finances, though the most recent evidence suggests the popularity of joint accounts.
- Some men argue their rights have been eroded, creating a crisis in masculinity.
- Neil Lyndon's solution to the 'sex war' was that each parent should work half time and take responsibility for the children the rest of the week.
- Conjugal-role studies fail to represent current family diversity.

- Childhood has developed as a distinct phase of life, different from adulthood, as a result of social changes.
- Childhood may be 'disappearing' again, as children grow up 'too fast' or they may be overprotected.
- As children are future parents and citizens, the current inquiry into the state of childhood is important.

Task 7.5

Answer this short examination-style question.

Identify and briefly explain two reasons for the emergence of the modern construction of childhood. (8 marks)

Guidance

- Though you should now be capable of entering into a full debate about whether childhood has 'disappeared', this short question is not inviting you to assess the situation. Instead, a simpler, factual approach is required (AO1), but good planning is essential.
- Before you write anything, think of two distinctively different reasons for conceptions of childhood changing since about the eighteenth century. Most candidates who lose marks do so because their reasons overlap. Each reason should be presented in a separate paragraph to help the examiner.
- For each reason, think of a key phrase, such as 'the introduction of compulsory education'. Follow this with no more than two or three sentences explaining how this factor made a difference.

Recommended websites

- Fathers 4 Justice
  http://fathers-4-justice.org
- UK Men and Fathers' Rights Organisation — extreme views on discrimination against men
  www.coeffic.demon.co.uk/descrim.htm
- BBC site relating to the series 'The Invention of Childhood' with many interesting links
  www.bbc.co.uk/radio4/history/childhood/
- A varied website on childhood despite its narrow-sounding title, 'The Philosophy of Childhood'
  http://plato.stanford.edu/entries/childhood/

Further reading

- Montgomery, H., Burr, R. and Woodhead, M. (eds) (2003) *Changing Childhoods, Local and Global*, Open University.
- Palmer, S. (2006) *Toxic Childhood: How the Modern World is Damaging Our Children and What We Can Do About It*, Orion Books.

Glossary

agency
  the individual's ability to make choices in life

cereal packet family
  a conventional family portrayed by advertisers; consists of white parents living with their own children, usually one boy and one girl

cohabitation
  an unmarried couple living together

conjugal roles
  tasks undertaken by husbands and wives

consensual union
  a couple cohabiting

conventional family
  a nuclear family in which the breadwinner father is married to the housewife mother

crisis in masculinity
  as females have taken advantage of increasing equal opportunities and become more successful in education and careers, while still being viewed as the central figure within the home, some men have felt their roles diminish

double shift
  responsibility for both paid and domestic work

expressive role
  caring and nurturing

extended family
  two or more nuclear families living under a single roof or in adjacent buildings

familism
  the promotion of conventional families

family diversity
  a variety of family structures, such as nuclear, single-parent and gay families

hegemony
  controlling people through ideas rather than physical force

household
a single person or a group occupying a house and cooperating economically

ideology of romance
the view that love and marriage should be a female priority

instrumental role
performing a practical means to an end, such as being a breadwinner

joint conjugal roles
the shared tasks of husbands and wives

kibbutz
an agricultural collective in Israel, whose main features include communal living, collective ownership of all property and the communal rearing of children

liberal feminists
feminists who believe gender equality can be achieved by legislation and the gradual softening of attitudes through education and the media

matrifocal
mother-headed

matrilineal
relating to female lines of descent

modified elementary family
term coined by Graham Allan (1985); a type of family where the sense of obligation in crises extends only to inner or 'elementary' members, not to uncles, cousins and more distant kin

modified extended family
term coined by Eugene Litwak (1975); this type of family differs from a classic family living together, but involves regular support and contact by telephone, post and visits (and, nowadays, e-mail and text messaging on mobile phones)

neo-conventional
a family differing from the conventional family only by the mother doing paid work

new man
a man willing to take on traditionally female roles

nuclear family
a man and a woman and their offspring

patriarchy
the dominance of society by older males

polyandry
the marriage of one woman to several husbands

polygamy
marriage to more than one partner at the same time

polygyny
the marriage of one man to several wives

post-feminism
a recent attitude that is resistant or indifferent to the pursuit of women's rights

radical feminists
feminists who believe that only drastic changes at the roots of society will help women

reconstituted family
a household from which one biological parent has departed and children live with the other biological parent and his or her new partner

re-formed family
see **reconstituted family**; also known as blended, reconfigured or step family

reserve army of labour
workers willing to fill jobs when they arise but dismissed easily during slumps

second wave feminism
movement for women's rights in the 1960s and 1970s

segregated gender roles
different tasks undertaken by men and women

socially constructed
a concept reflecting society's attitudes, as opposed to a natural phenomenon

stratified diffusion
lifestyle changes beginning in higher social classes and permeating down the social scale

structuration
the combined influence of social structure and choice of action on individual behaviour

symmetrical family

> both partners share responsibility for earning money, household chores and childcare, though sometimes performing different tasks

third wave or difference feminism

> a movement for rights of specific groups of women

triple shift

> responsibility for paid work, housework and emotional support